CW01263979

THE LOTUS BOOK

TYPE 1 TO TYPE 72

ISBN 1 84155 623 8

COLIN PITT, LLB

FOREWORD BY LEN TERRY

THE ESSENTIAL GUIDE TO HISTORIC LOTUS CARS

ISBN: 1 84155 623 8

Typeset by Planagraphics, Rayleigh, Essex from a handwritten manuscript.

Printed in Great Britain by HSW Print 01443 441100

Publishers: CP Press, PO Box 2795, Hockley, Essex SS5 4BY. England.

First Published in July 2005.

CONTENTS

ACKNOWLEDGEMENTS

Photographs have come from a variety of sources and I am particularly grateful to the Ludvigsen Library and Karl Ludvigsen, the Indianapolis Motor Speedway Library and Mary Ellen Loscar, Ferret Photographics and Ted Walker, and the LAT Library and Cathy Agar and Tim Wright. Thanks also to Victor Thomas of the Historic Lotus Register, the Ford Motor Company, Jutta Fausel, and to anyone else who has rendered assistance with photographs or otherwise. Bill Vincent lent great assistance with chassis numbers on the Mark VIII and additional photographic shots were provided by Maurice Rowe.

Many publications have been useful cross-references for these vehicles including Ian Smith's "Lotus the Story of the Marque," Doug Nye's "Single Seat Lotus Formula 1 and Indy", Andrew Ferguson's "Team Lotus", Anthony Pritchard's "Lotus All the Cars" and Michael Oliver's "Lotus 49" these being the leading books on the Lotus marque.

Lastly thanks to Ji-Ji for her help with magazines and annuals, and to my father Anthony Pitt who first met Colin Chapman whilst working on the Lotus Type 28.

Colin Pitt LLB, 2005

FOREWORD

Much has been written over the years about the marque Lotus and deservedly so for there is little doubt that Anthony Colin Bruce Chapman was the outstanding automotive designer of his day.

The wide range of cars covered in this book illustrates that fact perfectly, from the Mk 1 with thirty or so horse-power to some of the later models with something approaching one thousand hp, and from trials cars through front and mid-engined road-going coupes to World Championship and Indy winners as well as most of the other Formulae. They are all here and I believe that this is the first time that they have all been covered in the same volume.

A worthy contribution to the documentation of Lotus history. During the period 1958 to 1976 I was employed by Team Lotus for a total of about five years both as a member of staff and as a free-lance. For me it was always an education and whilst so employed I was involved one way and another with 21 of the 71 models mentioned in the following pages.

Although Colin and I were never "best buddies" and didn't always see eye to eye with one another I feel that, in the main, we worked extremely well together and were a very good pairing with my practicality making a perfect foil for his ingenuity and I like to believe that I played a small but significant part in the legend that is Lotus.

Len Terry.

MARK I MARK II MARK III MARK IV MARK VI

Colin Chapman's Lotus Mark I was built while he was serving in the RAF. It was Austin-Seven based and was produced primarily for participation in reliability trials. While still serving in the RAF, Colin Chapman was running the Mark I in trials during week-end leaves.

Another Lotus Trials Car followed, the Mark II which utilised a Ford Ten engine as the power-unit. One novel feature of the Lotus Mark II was a "jelly-joint", a device that Colin Chapman decided upon after spending considerable time studying tractor front suspension systems. Tractor front wheels will "pick their way" over the roughest ground.

Colin Chapman abandoned trials when the "750 formula" was announced in 1950. Chapman's car, the Lotus Mark III was built during the winter of 1950-1961, and was built to comply with the 750 formula. The Mark III's first race appearance was at Castle Combe early in May 1951. Onto the Mark III chassis an aluminium body was fitted which was made by local firm F. L. Hine & Co.

Colin Chapman with friends Michael and Nigel Allen managed to extract more power from the 747 cc side valve engine of the Mark III by modifying the inlet manifolds. The 750 Motor Club subsequently prohibited the dividing of the siamezed inlet ports.

From 1 January 1952 Colin Chapman entered into partnership with Michael Allen and they formed Lotus Engineering Company. The Lotus Mark IV was made as an order for Mike Lawson. Lawson used the car in competitions until the end of 1954. As delivered to Mike Lawson the Mark IV (registered LMU 4) had a single carburettor. Another modification to Lawson's car was the removal of the "jelly-joint" a fitting of a conventional Ford Beam Axle. The first major event for Lawson's Mark IV was the Colmore Trophy Trial on 22 March 1952, a championship event, in which the fourth best performance of the day was achieved. At West Hants Motor Club Knott Cup Trials on 20th September 1952 the Mark IV was fifth best. At the end of 1952 in the RAC Trials Championship the

Mark IV finished fifth. On 20th November 1954 Mike Lawson won the Roy Fedden Trophy in the Bristol Motor Club event.

The Lotus Mark VI was the first all Lotus chassis designed by Colin Chapman. Due to pressure of work only two Lotus Mark VIs were produced in 1952.

The Mark VI received all sorts of power units and over one hundred cars were built. Doug Chivas drove the first Mark VI to reach Australia, while Tom Gilmour had the first Lotus Mark VI to be imported into Canada. Gilmour's car had a 1500 MGTF engine. Bill Klinck from the USA also raced an MG engined version.

The first Lotus Mark VI was registered XML 6. Unfortunately while Nigel Allen was driving this vehicle to their first international race meeting it collided with a bread van and the car was written off. The suspension units fitted to the Lotus Mark VI are of the co-axial coilspring/ telescopic damper type and are manufactured by Woodhead Monroe. The Lotus Mark VI braking systems of the

Peter Gammon's "UPE 9" powered by a 1497cc MG engine became well known at race meetings. During 1954 he won the Performance Car Trophy. It won more awards than any other 1500 cc car during 1954.

who was works driver to both Porsche and Mercedes Benz. The Porsche 550 had to make do with 3rd place. Other Lotus successes in this race included 4th place (Coombs), 9th place (Anthony) and 23rd place (Manwaring). Fastest lap time was achieved by Peter Gammon at 84.30 mph.

Ken Laverton and John Lawry stayed with the 1172cc Ford engine in their Mark VI cars and had numerous wins. John Lawry won the 1200 cc class of the Autosport Series Production Sports Car Championship in 1956.

single cable type, with one inner and one outer cable only. The steering gear used on the Lotus Mark VI is of the Burnman worm and nut type, similar to that used on the Ford Popular. The side-valve engine normally used in the Lotus Mark VI is the Ford Ten E93A unit.

By 1954 Lotus had achieved much success. At the International "Daily Express" Trophy Meeting on 15 May 1954 in the Sports Car Race Colin Chapman came 15th, Peter Gammon came 20th, and Mike Anthony came 23rd all with the 1467 cc Lotus. In the Sports Car Race at Silverstone on 17th July 1954 Colin Chapman in his Lotus Mark VIII gained 1st place in a time of 36 minutes and 32 seconds. In 2nd place was Peter Gammon in a Lotus Mark VI in a time of 36 minutes and 48 seconds. Both beat the Porsche driven by Hans Herrmann

LOTUS MARK VI
SPECIFICATIONS

ENGINE:
Ford Consul side-valve 1099 cc

GEARBOX:
Ford three-speed

CHASSIS:
Multi tubular space-frame

DIMENSIONS:

Wheelbase	7ft 3-5 inches
Front track	49 inches
Rear track	45 inches
Overall length	121 inches
Overall width	51.5 inches
Scuttle height	30.5 inches

WEIGHT:
8.5 cwts

LOTUS SEVEN AND SUPER SEVEN

The Lotus Seven Series III

LOTUS SEVEN 1100 cc COVENTRY CLIMAX 1958 SPECIFICATIONS

BRAKES:
9.5 inch Girling discs

TYRE SIZE:

Front 4.50 x 15	Rear 5.00 x 15

GEAR RATIOS:

1st	2.5 to 1
2nd	1.67 to 1
3rd	1.23 to 1
Top	1 to 1,
Reverse	2.5 to 1,
Final drive ratio	4.9 to 1

ENGINE:

Bore	72.4mm
Stroke	66.6mm
Cubic capacity	1098
Compression ratio	9.8 to 1
Power output	80bhp at 6800 rpm

DIMENSIONS:

Wheelbase	7ft 4 inches
Front track	3ft 11 inches
Rear track	3ft 11 inches
Overall length	10ft 3 inches
Overall width	4ft 5 inches
Height to scuttle	2ft 3.5 inches
Ground clearance	5 inches

The Lotus Seven, and the spelling is Seven not Mark 7, was a very up-to-date machine with multi-tube "space-frame", ultra-low build and exceptional road holding and handling.

Independent front "swing-axle" suspension that was for so long a feature of the Lotus machine has gone and in its place a coil spring/damper-wishbone anti-roll bar layout.

In the standard model a BMC rear axle replaces the Ford axle used on the Mark VI. Like the Mark VI the power-unit usually specified is the 1172 cc side-valve Ford Anglia/prefect engine. The three speed Ford gearbox was fitted with a special Buckler second gear, which transforms the box into a close-ratio unit permitting speeds of nearly 75 mph to be reached in second, making overtaking a certain and delightful business.

The gear-change is effected by a lever mounted on the propeller-shaft tunnel where it falls conveniently to hand. Brakes are Girling hydraulic outboard drums all-round with 9 inch by 1.75 inch diameter at the front, and 8 inch by 1.25 inch at the rear. The rear mounted 7 gallon fuel tank gives the car a range of approximately 210 miles under fast driving conditions.

The Lotus Super Seven has quite a pedigree, its antecendents running back through the current Mark Seven models to the earlier Lotus Seven MK I and the original Lotus Mark VI. A background then, of thoroughly tried, tested and developed sports cars. The characteristic Lotus approach was no soft suspension nor comfortable seats but cars which gave real sports car motoring, cars which were either chosen for their performance or not at all.

The Lotus Super Seven weighs about 8.5 cwt and is powered by an 80 bhp Cosworth-Ford Classic engine. The power to weight ratio is pretty impressive. It works out at over 200 bhp per ton. The car could just reach 100 mph on a flat straight, with just over 6000 rpm on the clock. Acceleration is shattering and the ability to accelerate strongly is maintained right up to 80 plus mph.

The braking system of the Lotus Super Seven is based on a normal hydraulic drum layout, and sports competition linings. Performance figures for the Lotus Super Seven include 0-30 mph in 2.5 seconds, 0-60 mph in 7.6 seconds and a standing quarter mile in 16 seconds. Maximum speed is 102 mph at 6200 rpm.

LOTUS SUPER SEVEN SPECIFICATIONS

ENGINE:
Cosworth-Ford classic 109E
1340 cc ohv
Two twin-choke weber DCOE 40
carburettors

TRANSMISSION:
Four speed Ford Box with optional close-ratio gears

CHASSIS:
Space Frame, wishbone and coil spring front suspension, with anti-roll bar. Live axle rear, located by trailing arms. Coil spring dampers. Rack and pinion steering.

DIMENSIONS:
Wheelbase	7ft 4 inches
Track	4ft 0.5 inches
Weight	8 cwt 64 lbs
Overall length	11ft 0 inches
Overall width	4ft 10.75 inches

Lotus 7 GTS

Other Lotus Seven cars included the Lotus Seven A, the Lotus Seven A America, the Lotus Seven F, and the Lotus Super Seven 1500. The Lotus Seven SS had a twin-cam engine by Holbay. The Lotus Seven Series 3 made only between 1968 and 1970 was the car that came back in improved form as the Lotus Caterham Seven.

MARK 8

For the Lotus Mark VIII Frank Costin designed the body and Colin Chapman designed a new triangulated "space-frame" of 1.25 inch, 20-gauge steel tubing which would provide the utmost rigidity but without any needless excess weight. Frank Costin had been an aerodynamicist with the de Havilland Aircraft Company. The prototype was built during the winter of 1953-1954. A 1.5 litre engine built up of both MGTC and Morris 10 components was chosen as the power-unit. With a power-output of around 85 bhp, wind-tunnel testing estimated that the car would reach in excess of 125 mph.

Stopping such a car from high speed would require something different in the way of brakes. Among the special features of the the Lotus Mark VIII was a semi-monocoque-type of body panelling. This gave quite an advantage in weight saving.

"SAR 5" kept its date for appearance at Brands Hatch on the 8th April 1954 but only gained 4th place in the 1500 cc National Sports Car Championship.

At the front of the Lotus Mark VIII the well-known divided axle front suspension is retained, controlled by helical springs and Woodhead-Monroe hydraulic dampers. At the rear a de Dion type of axle is used, in conjunction with a transverse helical spring held in tension, and damped by Armstrong piston-type units. Lotus Mark VIII were also built for Dick Steed, "Tip" Cunane and Brian Naylor.

At Brands Hatch on 4th July 1954, Colin Chapman had to make do with coming second to Peter Gammon who won the 1500 cc Sports Car Races. By the end of 1954 "SAR 5" had become the quickest 1.5 litre MG powered car in the country.

Lotus Mark VIII CHASSIS NUMBERS

CHASSIS NUMBER MK 8/01
REGISTRATION SAR 5

Known as P3 (prototype three) at the Lotus works. Lightweight 20 swg aluminium body shell by Williams & Pritchard. Raced extensively throughout 1954 by Colin Chapman. Sold to Austen Nurse for 1955, sold to Roy Bloxham for 1956, crashed by Bloxham at Mallory Park.

CHASSIS NUMBER MK6/2-1
REGISTRATION TYC 700

Delivered to George "Tip" Cunane after much delay in early 1955, less engine, and built up by his mechanic Eric Wilmott. The engine, supplied by BMC's competition department, was a special version of the 1466 cc MG XPEG pushrod unit as used in later MG TFs. Sold to Mr Dimmock in 1959, sold to Mr Stroud for 1961, sold to Richard Whittington in 1963 his planned restoration never took place and the car was sold to Dutchman Olaf Glassius. The car now fully restored remains in Holland.

CHASSIS NUMBER MK6/2-2
REGISTRATION 624 BMG

Production car built up by Nigel Allen with 18 swg Williams & Pritchard body shell. Raced extensively in UK and in Europe during 1954 and 1955 by Allen. Fitted with Ford torque tube rear axle. Modified MG TC engine with special Nigel Allen cylinder head and a pair of experimental Solex twin-choke carburettors that proved troublesome. Sold to Sir Jeremy Reilly 1956, who raced the car in Northern Ireland. Bought by Stan Verall in 1958 and used as a road car until 1962. Bought by the late Tony Codling in 1963 as a road car and used by him until sold privately in 1973.

CHASSIS NUMBER MK6/2-3
REGISTRATION 867 BMX

Production car delivered to Dan Maguilles. Raced throughout 1954 in UK and Europe; sold to Brian Naylor at the end of 1954 and Mark IX brake drums fitted at the works. Currently in the USA.

CHASSIS NUMBER MK6/2-4
REGISTRATION HUD 139

Production car delivered to Dickie Steed in August 1954. First Lotus to be powered by the new Coventry Climax FWA engine. Some racing successes during 1954; to Dave Kelsey in 1955 who raced it under the 1172 Formula regulations until the end of that year. Currently in the UK.

SAR5, now owned by Bill Vincent, won its class at the Daily Express International Race at Silverstone on 15th May 1954.

LOTUS MARK VIII SPECIFICATIONS

ENGINE:
Four cylinders, 72 mm x 90 mm
1467 cc Pushrod operated valves in light alloy head.
85 bhp at 6200 rpm
9 to 1 compression ratio.
Twin 1.75 inch SU carburettors

TRANSMISSION:
Borg and Beck racing clutch. Four-speed gearbox with central remote control and synchromesh on upper three gears. Open Hardy Spicer propeller shaft to chassis-mounted spiral bevel and differential unit.

CHASSIS:
Multi-tubular space frame. Independent front suspension by swing axles, helical springs, and telescopic dampers. Rear suspension by de Dion axle, bell cranks, single helical spring, and piston-type dampers. Lockheed hydraulic brakes in Al-fin drums.

DIMENSIONS:

Wheelbase	7ft 3.5 inches
Front track	4ft 0.5 inches
Rear track	3ft 11.5 inches
Weight	10.25 cwt

Lotus Mark VIII CHASSIS NUMBERS

CHASSIS NUMBER MK6/2-5 REGISTRATION KJA 91

Production car bought by John Coombs who transferred the engine from his AL/SR Connaught sports racing car. First appearance at the British Grand Prix meeting in July 1954. Sold to Brian Naylor in 1955. Currently in the UK.

CHASSIS NUMBER MK6/2-6 REGISTRATION 777 FRE

Production car delivered to George Nixon early in 1955. Major chassis differences from earlier Mk VIIIs to allow for the installation of the Turner Lea-Francis engine and Armstrong manual gearbox. Limited success during 1955 due to engine failures. Sold early 1956. Currently in the UK.

CHASSIS NUMBER UNKNOWN REGISTRATION SXB 500

Believed to have come out the "back-door" of Lotus or one of its suppliers in 1955. Built as a road car and never seen at any race meeting. Earlier MK 6 chassis with Ford mechanics. Scrapped 1967.

In 1956 the above car, "SAR 5" was purchased by Roy Bloxam. Mrs Bloxham also competed in it regularly. After an accident at Mallory Park the car reappeared without the tail fins.

MARK 9

During the winter of 1954/55 Colin Chapman resigned from his job with the British Aluminium Company and became Managing Director of Lotus Engineering Company Limited. Mike Costin left the DeHavilland Aircraft Company and became a director of Racing Engines Limited. By splitting production between Lotus Engineering Company Limited and Racing Engines Limited, one supplying the chassis and the other the body, it was possible to avoid Purchase Tax.

The Lotus Mark IX is similar in appearance to its predecessor but to reduce drag and weight the overall length is reduced by approximately two feet and the height by five inches.

The chassis frame is of the space type, built up from round and square section mild steel tubes, a form of structure which has been proved in racing to be more suitable than the previously used nickel steel.

On the Lotus Mark IX the brake drums are turbo finned and made of magnesium alloy into which is cast an inner lining of iron. The rear brakes which incorporate similar drums, are fitted either side of the final drive assembly. On cars used for Le Mans and the Nine Hours of Goodwood disc brakes were used, which although causing a weight penalty guaranteed excellent braking.

The front suspension is independent, by means of a divided front axle, of Ford manufacture. The actual suspensory mediums are helical springs, the volutions of which surround the the Woodhead-Monroe hydraulic dampers. The rear suspension is again by helical springs, controlled by a de Dion tube, while lateral

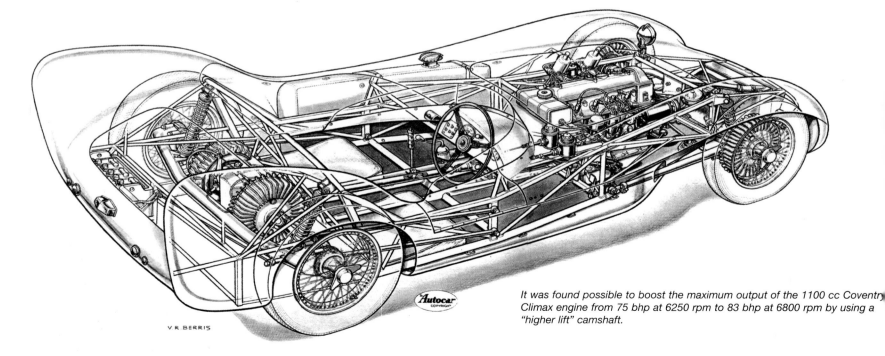

V.R. BERRIS

It was found possible to boost the maximum output of the 1100 cc Coventry Climax engine from 75 bhp at 6250 rpm to 83 bhp at 6800 rpm by using a "higher lift" camshaft.

Cutaway drawing of the 1955 Mark 9 by Vic Berris.

positioning of the assembly is by a Panhard rod. Ready to race, the car with driver and fuel weighs 11.6 cwt, which gives a power/weight ratio of roughly 130 bhp/ton compared to the previous year's car, the body is greatly improved. The vibration of the panels at high engine revolutions has been considerably reduced. In the case of the Climax-engined car one finds a well balanced machine where the power can be used nearly all the time.

Two cars with 1098 cc Coventry Climax FWA engine mated to a TC MG gearbox went to American owners Frank Miller and Norman Scott. In the Sebring 12 hours

LOTUS MARK IX CLIMAX SPECIFICATIONS

ENGINE:
Four cylinders 72.4 mm x 66.7 mm (1097 cc)
Single overhead camshaft operating valves in light alloy head.
81 bhp at 6700 rpm.
9.8 to 1 compression ratio.
Twin S.V. carburettors.

CHASSIS:
Multi-tubular space frame. Independent front suspension by swing axles. Rear suspension by de Dion axle. Helical springs and telescopic dampers.

DIMENSIONS:
Wheelbase	7ft 3.5 inches
Front Track	4ft 0.5 inches
Rear Track	3ft 11.5 inches
Weight	8.25 cwt

Lotus Mark IX (XPE 6) at the Tourist Trophy in 1955.

Race when Samuelson took over from Scott he has blinding by the sun and left the road and the race. Miller's co-driver was disqualified for receiving a push start.

In the Goodwood Nine Hour Race the car of R.A. Page and Paul Emery completed 268 laps, placing it eleventh overall and fourth in the 1500 cc class. Peter Ashdown won the 1500 cc Sports Car

Standing quarter-mile	*15.8 seconds*
0-60 mph	*7.8 seconds*
Maximum speed	*127.7 mph*
Price without engine and gearbox	*£850*

Race at KarlsKoga, Sweden while Peter Lumsden won the 1956 BARC Brooklands Trophy.

The Lotus Mark VIII had been aimed at a sports racing class of cars up to 1500 cc but quite often Mark VIIIs were mixing with larger engined cars such as the 2-litre Bristol engined cars. A constant adversary of Colin Chapman in his Mark VIII (SAR 5) was Scotsman Archie Scott-Brown. Scott-Brown's rise to prominence began in 1954 when he formed a partnership with entrant Brian Lister. In the Lister-Bristol Archie Scott-Brown proved a top contender and as a driver of sports cars he had few equals.

Requests, therefore, for a Lotus that would take a 2-litre engine started to come in from the likes of Peter Scott-Russell and Cliff Davis. Colin Chapman then set about modifying the Mark VIII chassis to take the large six-cylinder Bristol engine. Chassis modifications were extensive, but the normal Mark IX de Dion axle tube was retained and new Dunlop disc brakes were fitted at the front and mounted inboard on the differential at the rear. Williams & Pritchard built the body in 18-gauge aluminium alloy.

The Lotus Bristol was never intended as a new model of Lotus as it was in fact a modified and more powerful Mark VIII. At Goodwood in April 1955, in the sports cars up to 2000 cc race Mike Anthony came third in the Mark X behind Archie Scott-Brown in the Lister Bristol.

LOTUS MARK X SPECIFICATIONS

ENGINE:
Bristol six-cylinder

GEARBOX:
Bristol Four-speed

CUBIC CAPACITY:
1971 cc

CHASSIS:
Multi-tubular space-frame

FRONT SUSPENSION:
Swing axles and coil spring/damper units

REAR SUSPENSION:
de Dion axle and coil spring/damper units

DIMENSIONS:

Wheelbase	7ft 3.5 inches
Front track	4ft 0.5 inches
Rear track	3ft 11.5 inches
Weight	11 cwt

The new chassis frame of the Lotus Eleven followed the general principles of the Mark 9 Lotus in that main steel tubes were 1 inch diameter and subsidiary ones of 0.75 inch size in 18 or 20-gauge sections according to the work they had to do. So as to reduce weight the transmission tunnel was made into a stressed member and made from 20-gauge strong aircraft alloy sheet. This stressed section was to take the final drive torque reaction, part of the floor load and give support to the rear engine mounting.

A difference of the Eleven compared to the Mark 9 was that the Girling helical spring units which encircled hydraulic telescopic dampers were shorter than those used on the Mark 9 and were mounted closer to the centre line of the car. Also on the Eleven a "Le Mans" de Dion layout was used at the rear which saved ten unsprung pounds from the layout used on the Mark 9.

Two new Lotus Elevens appeared for the first time in Britain on 2nd April 1956. This was at the Goodwood Easter Monday meeting. Team Lotus driver Reg Bicknell driving a car powered by the 1460 cc engine managed 4th place in the up to 1500 cc sports car race.

At the April Brands Hatch Meeting Graham Hill won the up to 1200 cc sports car race and finished second to Reg Bicknell in the 1500 cc Team Lotus car in the up to 1500 cc race. Graham Hill recorded the fastest lap in the 1500 cc race at the speed of 72-73 mph which was a 1500cc class record.

On Whit Monday, 1956 there was an epic struggle between Colin Chapman and Mike Hawthorn in the up to 1500 cc Sports Car Race at Goodwood. On the 12th lap Mike Hawthorn had to pull into the pits enabling Colin Chapman to win. Team Lotus had a good day as Cliff Allison won the 1100 cc class.

At Aintree 1956 Graham Hill was driving the first of the "Sports" models in the Sports Car Race and won at the speed of 71.24 mph with a Ford 10 engine.

On 7th July 1956 Reg Bicknell drove his 1500 cc car to a fine victory at Mallory Park in the sports car race.

Hornsey had been desperately trying to produce a special "record-breaker" Eleven for Stirling Moss to attack International Class G records at Monza on Monday 3rd September 1956. This was the day after the European Grand Prix.

The rush had been due to last minute availability of the high speed track. Because of the hurry a purely standard car was used but with a completely enveloping "bubble" cockpit being added. A Stage 2 1100 cc Coventry Climax engine was installed but instead of using normal SU carburettors, a pair of Weber twin-choke units were fitted. Slightly larger tyres than usual were fitted.

Record attempts started in the early morning and a 50 km record at 135.54 mph (218.12 kph) and a 50-mile record at 132.77 mph (213.66 kph) had been established. Attempts were halted when the rear sub-frame fractured and the tail of the car parted from the rest at high speed.

Further attempts were made on 2nd October and 9th October with Mackay Fraser driving. New records were set. 50 km at 138 mph, 50 miles at 138 mph, 100 km at 137.2 mph, 100 miles at 137,5 mph, 200 km at 137.5 mph and 1 hour at 137.5 mph. Fastest flying lap was 143 mph and an incredible speed for an unblown 1100cc sports car.

A good start to the year came when on 13th February 1957 Colin Chapman was awarded the Ferodo Gold Trophy for outstanding British contribution to motor racing in 1956. The 1957 Eleven was to resemble the 1956 car but Colin Chapman was keen to incorporate wishbone front suspension and to make alterations to the rear-end so the power of the twin-cam 1500 cc engine could be accommodated. The main change to enable this was to increase the 18-gauge de Dion tube from 3 inch diameter to 3.625 inch diameter. A prototype chassis was commenced on these lines. This new car bore chassis number 300, showing the number of cars the small factory had produced in four

years since the first production Mark 6. On a basic chassis it was now possible to have four distinct Elevens. First came the Sports 45 with Ford Engine, live rear-axle and drum brakes, second came the Club 75 with Climax engine replacing the Ford, third came the Le Mans 85 with the de Dion and disc brakes and fourthly the Le Mans 150 with twin overhead camshaft engine. The basic prices of these four models when bought complete were Le Mans 150- £2885, Le Mans 85 – £1690, Club 75 – £1309, Sports 45 – £1021. At the Sebring 12 Hour in March 1957 Colin Chapman, Joe Shepphard and Dick Dungan's Lotus Lotus Eleven gained eleventh place while at the Le Mans 24 Hours in June 1957 Herbert MacKay-

Fraser and Jay Chamberlain gained ninth place after completing 285 laps. Also in the Le Mans race of 1957 Robert Walshaw and John Dalton gained thirteenth place after completing 259 laps and Keith Hall and Cliff Allison made fourteenth place after completing 259 laps. Roger Masson and Andre Hechard completed the positions of Lotus Elevens in the race with sixteenth place after completing 253 laps.

Lotus Eleven at Le Mans 1957

LOTUS ELEVEN RACING RECORD

DATE	EVENT	CAR NO.	DRIVERS	LAPS COMPLETED	RACE RESULT
28th-29th July 1956	Le Mans 24 Hrs	36	Reg Bicknell Peter Jopp	253	7th
28th-29th July 1956	Le Mans 24 Hrs	35	Cliff Allison Keith Hall	89	Did not finish (Accident)
28th-29th July 1956	Le Mans 24 Hrs	32	Colin Chapman Herbert Mackay-Fraser	172	Did not finish (Engine)
23rd March 1957	Sebring 12 Hrs	59	Colin Chapman Joe Sheppard Dick Dungan	174	11th
23rd March 1957	Sebring 12 Hrs	61	Victor Merino Luis Pedrerra Rafael Rosales	141	32nd
23rd March 1957	Sebring 12 Hrs	74	M.R.J Wyllie Margaret Wyllie Charles Moran	89	Did not finish (Disqualified)
23rd March 1957	Sebring 12 Hrs	60	Jay Chamberlain Ignacio Lozano	77	Did not finish (Fuel Leak)
26th May 1957	Nürburgring 1000 kms	33	David Piper N.R. Hicks Anthony J. Hogg	34	19th
26th May 1957	Nürburgring 1000 kms	32	William Frost Mike .P. Anthony	17	Did not finish (Accident)
26th May 1957	Nürburgring 1000 kms	34	Anthony J. Hogg David Piper	7	Did not finish (Accident)
26th May 1957	Nürburgring 1000 kms	36	Herbert Mackay Fraser Dan Margulies Anthony J. Hogg	3	Did not finish (Axle)
22nd-23rd June 1957	Le Mans 24 Hrs	62	Herbert Mackay Fraser Jay Chamberlain	285	9th
22nd-23rd June 1957	Le Mans 24 Hrs	42	Robert Walshaw John Dalton	259	13th
22nd-23rd June 1957	Le Mans 24 Hrs	55	Keith Hall Cliff Allison	259	14th
22nd-23rd June 1957	Le Mans 24 Hrs	41	Roger Masson Andre Hechard	253	16th

LOTUS ELEVEN RACING RECORD

DATE	EVENT	CAR NO.	DRIVERS	LAPS COMPLETED	RACE RESULT
11th August 1957	Swedish G.P.	35	Cliff Allison Innes Ireland	115	18th
11th August 1957	Swedish G.P.	36	Peter Ashdown Alan Stacey	100	Not running at finish
11th August 1957	Swedish G.P.	27	William Frost Mike P. Anthony	91	Not running at finish
3rd November 1957	Venezuelan G.P.	78	Luis Ojanguren Peter Monteverdi	23	Did not finish
22nd March 1958	Sebring 12 Hrs	56	Sam Weiss Dave Tallakson	179	4th
22nd March 1958	Sebring 12 Hrs	55	Colin Chapman Cliff Allison	179	6th
22nd March 1958	Sebring 12 Hrs	54	Jay Chamberlain William Frost	175	9th
22nd March 1958	Sebring 12 Hrs	49	Charles Moran Paul Ceresole	110	Not classified
1st June 1958	Nürburgring 1000 kms	29	David Piper Keith Greene	38	15th
1st June 1958	Nürburgring 1000 kms	36	John Horridge Walter E. Monaco	29	Did not finish
1st June 1958	Nürburgring 1000 kms	28	Jimmy Blumer Walter Christopher Power	6	Did not finish
21st-22nd June 1958	Le Mans 24 Hrs	55	Alan Stacey Tom Dickson	202	Not classified
21st-22nd June 1958	Le Mans 24 Hrs	38	Innes Ireland Mike Taylor	162	Did not finish
21st-22nd June 1958	Le Mans 24 Hrs	39	N. Robert Hicks William Frost	28	Did not finish
13th September 1958	Tourist Trophy	42	Peter Ashdown Gordon Jones	138	7th
13th September 1958	Tourist Trophy	46	Mike Taylor Keith Greene	134	10th
13th September 1958	Tourist Trophy	50	Henry Taylor Nicholas Green	131	11th

LOTUS ELEVEN RACING RECORD

DATE	EVENT	CAR NO.	DRIVERS	LAPS COMPLETED	RACE RESULT
13th September 1958	Tourist Trophy	27	William Frost Richard Stoop	128	13th
13th September 1958	Tourist Trophy	47	Jack Westcott Peter Arundell	125	15th
13th September 1958	Tourist Trophy	41	Alan Stacey Keith Hall	121	17th
13th September 1958	Tourist Trophy	48	Douglas Graham Christopher Martyn	110	18th
13th September 1958	Tourist Trophy	52	Jimmy Blumer C. Stuart Dodd	99	Not classified
13th September 1958	Tourist Trophy	24	Bruce McLaren Syd H.Jensen	53	Did not finish
13th September 1958	Tourist Trophy	26	David Shale John Dalton	24	Did not finish
13th September 1958	Tourist Trophy	53	John Fisher Les Leston	20	Did not finish
13th September 1958	Tourist Trophy	25	Edward G.Greenall John Campbell-Jones	9	Did not finish
21st March 1959	Sebring 12 Hrs	40	Charles Moran George Rand	145	33rd
21st March 1959	Sebring 12 Hrs	47	Thomas T.Fleming Bill Schade	123	Not classified
7th June 1959	Nürburgring 1000 kms	43	John Campbell-Jones John Horridge	39	16th
7th June 1959	Nürburgring 1000 kms	41	Jacques Lefebvre Walter E. Monaco	35	37th
5th September 1959	Tourist Trophy	39	John Campbell-Jones John Horridge	154	Not classified
5th September 1959	Tourist Trophy	40	Peter Arundell Jack Westcott	-	Did not finish
12th May 1963	Spa-Francorchamps	8	John F. Dickinson	27	22nd
12th May 1963	Spa-Francorchamps	3	Adriende Ghellinck	13	Did not finish

Use of wishbones at the front of the Lotus 12 was a new departure for Lotus when it was introduced at the 1956 Earl's Court Motor Show

LOTUS TYPE 12 SPECIFICATIONS

ENGINE:
Coventry Climax FPF

CAPACITY:
1475, 1960 or 2207 cc

GEARBOX:
Lotus Five-Speed

POWER OUTPUT:
141 bhp, 175 bhp or 194 bhp

DIMENSIONS:
Wheelbase	7ft 4 inches
Front Track	48 inches
Rear Track	48 inches
Tip to nose length	10ft 11 inches

CHASSIS:
Multi-tubular space-frame

STEERING:
Rack and Pinion

BODY:
Aluminium by Williams & Pritchard

WEIGHT:
6 cwt

A prototype was tested at Silverstone in March 1957, but the Lotus Type 12 made its debut at the Goodwood Easter Monday with Cliff Allison at the wheel. Cliff Allison's second place at the Oulton Park Gold Cup was probably about the best result of the year with a Lotus Type 12. The car had bottom chassis longerons which were made in aircraft specification Reynolds 531 tube. Curved inch square cross members linked the main longerons. The engine was mounted by using a rear engine place of 10 - gauge alloy fitted as a bulkhead at four points..

Of the twelve Lotus Twelve's built the first prototype 351, was destroyed after crashing in the 1960 Australian Grand Prix. Chassis 350 was the prototype and 1956 Motor Show car. Other chassis numbers for Lotus 12 were 352, 353, 354, 355, 356, 357, 358, 359, 360 and 361. The frame of chassis 359, owned by Ivor Bueb in 1958, carries the number F2-3-58 stamped near the gear change quadrant. In April 1958 Cliff Allison (357) and Graham Hill (353) entered the Glover Trophy, in May 1958 Graham Hill (353) entered Silverstone International Trophy.

Also in May 1958 Cliff Allison (357) and Graham Hill (353) entered the Monaco G.P., and later that month in the same cars Allison and Hill entered in the Dutch G.P. In June 1958, Allison (357) and Hill (353) entered the Belgian G.P. Only Allison (357) entered the Reims G.P. in July 1958 and the British G.P., and Italian G.P. in September 1958. Cliff Allison was the sole entrant for the October 1958 Moroccan G.P.

LOTUS TYPE 14 SPECIFICATIONS

FRAME:

Integral chassis/body structure of glass-reinforced Epoxide and Polyester resin. This gives advantages of exceptional strength, very good impact resistance, sound damping and good thermal insulation.

POWER UNIT:

Single ohc Coventry Climax 4 cylinder engine bore and stroke 76.2 mm x 66.6 mm = 1229 cc Maximum power output 75 bhp at 6100 rpm. The compression ratio is 8.5 to 1. The engine is water-cooled and has a steel crankshaft of fully counter-weighted design with a large overlap between crankpins and main journals, carried in three 2.125 inch diameter and 1 inch wide main bearings of lead-bronze steel backed thin strip type. The aluminium pistons are fitted with plated top rings High mechanical efficiency is provided by a piston speed of 2500 ft/min at 5750 rpm. Cylinder head is heat-treated aluminium. There is a chain drive from jackshaft to camshaft.

PRODUCED:

At least 988 and the prototype was assumed to be chassis no.1000

DIMENSIONS:

Wheelbase	7ft 4 inches
Front track	3ft 11 inches
Rear track	3ft 11 inches
Overall length	12 feet
Overall width	4ft 10 inches
Height to roof	3ft 10 inches
Minimum ground clearance	7 inches

The first person to hear of Colin Chapman's proposed coupe was Colin's friend Peter Kirwan-Taylor. The early design thought up by these two did not alter greatly despite te opinions of various experts. To keep the project as secret as possible Lotus took over a small assembly shop in Edmonton and it was here that John Frayling was in charge of sculptural work in the moulds for various units.

The structure of the car is made up basically of eight box sections. At the rear a triangular box provides attachment points for the final drive unit and suspension items. From this, four boxes travel forward as stressed sections, the main one being a deep propeller shaft tunnel. In production it was possible to impregnate the glass fibre with a colour as well as paint spraying for a final finish.

The standard Elite built at the factory cost just over £2000, but £631 of that was purchase tax. It was therefore possible to buy kits which could be put together by the inexperienced amateur in only 25 hours and save the purchase tax.

THE LOTUS ELITE'S LE MANS RECORD

1959	Peter Lumsden and Peter Riley	8th overall	1961	Kosselek and Massenet	13th overall
1959	Jim Clark and Sir John Whitmore	10th overall	1962	David Hobbs and Frank Gardner	8th overall
1960	Roger Masson and Claude Laurent	13th overall	1962	Clive Hunt and Dr John Wyllie	11th overall
1960	John Wagstaff and Tony Marsh	14th overall	1963	John Wagstaff and Pat Ferguson	10th overall
1961	Bill Allen and Trevor Taylor	12th overall	1964	John Wagstaff and Clive Hunt	22nd overall

Lotus Elites

LOTUS ELITE RACING RECORD

DATE	EVENT	CAR NO.	DRIVERS	LAPS COMPLETED	RACE RESULT
21st March 1959	Sebring 12 Hrs	45	Pete Lovely Jay Chamberlain Sam Weiss	160	21st
7th June 1959	Nürburgring 1000 kms	85	Peter Lumsden Peter Riley	38	23rd
20th-21st June 1959	Le Mans 24 Hrs	41	Peter Lumsden Peter Riley	270	8th
20th-21st June 1959	Le Mans 24 Hrs	42	Jim Clark John Whitmore	257	10th
20th-21st June 1959	Le Mans 24 Hrs	38	Jean-Claude Vidilles Jean-Francois Malle	105	Did not finish (Overheating)
26th March 1960	Sebring 12 Hrs	55	C.W. Evans Sam Weiss Jay Chamberlain	158	25th
26th March 1960	Sebring 12 Hrs	57	Frank Bott Phil Forno	57	Did not finish (Accident)
26th March 1960	Sebring 12 Hrs	56	Jim Hughes Sam Weiss	5	Did not finish (Fatal Accident)
22nd May 1960	Nürburgring 1000 kms	117	Alan Stacey John Wagstaff	39	20th
20th May 1960	Nürburgring 1000 kms	115	Peter Lumsden Peter Sargent	39	21st
20th May 1960	Nürburgring 1000 kms	121	George R. Kreisel Ed Shaffer	36	32nd
20th May 1960	Nürburgring 1000 kms	119	Mike Parkes Gawaine Baillie	28	Did not finish (Accident)
20th May 1960	Nürburgring 1000 kms	116	David Buxton W.E.J. Allen	26	Did not finish (Accident)
20th May 1960	Nürburgring 1000 kms	112	Andre Liekens Pascal Demol	14	Did not finish
25th-26th June 1960	Le Mans 24 Hrs	44	Roger Masson Claude Laurent	261	13th

LOTUS ELITE RACING RECORD

DATE	EVENT	CAR NO.	DRIVERS	LAPS COMPLETED	RACE RESULT
25th-26th June 1960	Le Mans 24 Hrs	41	John Wagstaff Tony Marsh	257	14th
25th-26th June 1960	Le Mans 24 Hrs	43	Mike Parkes Gawaine Baillie	169	Did not finish (Gearbox)
25th-26th June 1960	Le Mans 24 Hrs	42	David Buxton W.E.J. Allen	157	Did not finish (Clutch)
20th August 1960	Tourist Trophy	45	Peter Lumsden Chris Kerrison	102	9th
20th August 1960	Tourist Trophy	52	Graham Warner	102	10th
20th August 1960	Tourist Trophy	44	Chris Summers	100	12th
20th August 1960	Tourist Trophy	46	Mike Parkes	100	13th
20th August 1960	Tourist Trophy	49	John H. Gaston	97	17th
20th August 1960	Tourist Trophy	47	Sydney H. Hurrell Roy North	95	21st
20th August 1960	Tourist Trophy	41	W.E.J. Allen David Buxton	93	22nd
20th August 1960	Tourist Trophy	51	E.J.P. Williams Tony Hegbourne	91	23rd
20th August 1960	Tourist Trophy	43	Tony Marsh John Wagstaff	63	Did not finish
4th September 1960	Monza Coppa Inter-Europa	26	John Coundley	79	16th
4th September 1960	Monza Coppa Inter-Europa	24	Charles Voegele	61	Did not finish
28th May 1961	Nürburgring 1000 kms	90	Peter Lumsden Peter Riley	40	18th
28th May 1961	Nürburgring 1000 kms	92	David Hobbs Bill Pickney	40	20th
28th May 1961	Nürburgring 1000 kms	103	Bernd Degner Charly Braun	39	27th
28th May 1961	Nürburgring 1000 kms	98	W.E.J. Allen John Wagstaff	38	30th

LOTUS ELITE RACING RECORD

DATE	EVENT	CAR NO.	DRIVERS	LAPS COMPLETED	RACE RESULT
28th May 1961	Nürburgring 1000 kms	102	George R. Kreisel Scott Berridge	38	33rd
28th May 1961	Nürburgring 1000 kms	94	Les Leston Keith Ballisat	38	34th
28th May 1961	Nürburgring 1000 kms	97	Helmut Busch Joerg Schmitz	30	Not running at finish
28th May 1961	Nürburgring 1000 kms	93	Edward G. Greenall Ian B. Baillie	29	Did not finish
28th May 1961	Nürburgring 1000 kms	91	Ted Lund Norbert Hermann	25	Did not finish
28th May 1961	Nürburgring 1000 kms	96	Jan Johnson Yngve Nystrom	6	Did not finish
28th May 1961	Nürburgring 1000 kms	101	Paul Deetens Carl Smet	2	Did not finish
10th-11th June 1961	Le Mans 24 Hrs	38	W.E.J. Allen Trevor Taylor	268	12th
10th-11th June 1961	Le Mans 24 Hrs	40	Benard. Kosellek Pierre Massenez	267	13th
10th-11th June 1961	Le Mans 24 Hrs	39	M.R.J. Wyllie David Buxton	193	Did not finish
10th-11th June 1961	Le Mans 24 Hrs	51	Cliff Allison Mike McKee	102	Did not finish
10th-11th June 1961	Le Mans 24 Hrs	41	Jean Francois Malle Robin Carnegie	86	Did not finish
19th August 1961	Tourist Trophy	45	Les Leston	103	7th
19th August 1961	Tourist Trophy	47	Peter Lumsden Peter Riley	103	8th
19th August 1961	Tourist Trophy	41	W.E.J. Allen	102	9th
19th August 1961	Tourist Trophy	49	Peter Jopp	98	13th
19th August 1961	Tourist Trophy	48	Edward G. Greenall	98	14th

LOTUS ELITE RACING RECORD

DATE	EVENT	CAR NO.	DRIVERS	LAPS COMPLETED	RACE RESULT
19th August 1961	Tourist Trophy	46	John Whitmore Chris Barber	78	19th
19th August 1961	Tourist Trophy	43	Ted Lund Peter Sherman	56	Did not finish
19th August 1961	Tourist Trophy	42	Clive Hunt Trevor Taylor	26	Did not finish
19th August 1961	Tourist Trophy	44	Graham Warner	15	Did not finish
10th September 1961	Monza Coppa Inter-Europa	40	John Coundley	82	5th
11 February 1962	Daytona 3 hrs	30	Jim Clark	60	29th
11 February 1962	Daytona 3 hrs	48	William Storey Charlie Kolb	58	30th
11 February 1962	Daytona 3 hrs	27	Milo Vega Howard Franklin	51	Not classified
24th March 1962	Sebring 12 Hrs	68	Newton Davis Peter Pulver	155	29th
24th March 1962	Sebring 12 Hrs	69	Don Hulette Burk Wiedner	59	Did not finish
27th May 1962	Nürburgring 1000 kms	2	John Wagstaff J.Pat Fergusson	38	16th
23rd-24th June 1962	Le Mans 24 Hrs	44	David Hobbs Frank Gardner	286	8th
23rd-24th June 1962	Le Mans 24 Hrs	45	Clive Hunt M.R.J. Wyllie	278	11th
18th August 1962	Tourist Trophy	26	Clive Hunt	90	7th
18th August 1962	Tourist Trophy	27	Gil Baird Trevor Taylor	88	9th
18th August 1962	Tourist Trophy	30	Jon A. Derisley John Nicholson	83	13th
18th August 1962	Tourist Trophy	29	Dizzy Addicott Tom J. Threlfall	83	15th

LOTUS ELITE RACING RECORD

DATE	EVENT	CAR NO.	DRIVERS	LAPS COMPLETED	RACE RESULT
18th August 1962	Tourist Trophy	25	Trevor Taylor Gil Baird	74	17th
18th August 1962	Tourist Trophy	22	Les Leston	71	19th
18th August 1962	Tourist Trophy	28	John Coundley Michael W. MacQuaker	67	Not classified
18th August 1962	Tourist Trophy	24	John Whitmore	50	Did not finish
18th August 1962	Tourist Trophy	23	Peter Jopp	24	Did not finish
18th August 1962	Tourist Trophy	42	Jimmy Blumer	19	Did not finish
21st October 1962	Paris 1000 kms	37	John Wagstaff Gil Baird	115	10th
21st October 1962	Paris 1000 kms	36	Trevor Taylor Clive Hunt	30	Did not finish (Engine)
21st October 1962	Paris 1000 kms	53	Andre Welcker Firmin Dauwe	20	Did not finish
21st October 1962	Paris 1000 kms	52	Henri Quernette Gustave Gosselin	1	Did not finish (Engine)
17th February 1963	Daytona 3 hrs	48	Bill Story Ray Heppenstall	64	16th
23rd March 1963	Sebring 12 Hrs	67	John Bentley John Gordon	151	38th
23rd March 1963	Sebring 12 Hrs	66	Leon Lilley Ed Graham	149	39th
12th May 1963	Spa-Francorchamps 500 kms	10	J. Pat Fergusson	32	6th
12th May 1963	Spa-Francorchamps 500 kms	2	Jon A. Derisley	30	13th
12th May 1963	Spa-Francorchamps 500 kms	7	Jean-Marie Pierson	29	Not running at finish
12th May 1963	Spa-Francorchamps 500 kms	6	Andre Welcker	30	15th

LOTUS ELITE RACING RECORD

DATE	EVENT	CAR NO.	DRIVERS	LAPS COMPLETED	RACE RESULT
12th May 1963	Spa-Francorchamps 500 kms	9	Luc Beaulen	28	21st
12th May 1963	Spa-Francorchamps 500 kms	11	Clive Hunt	18	Did not finish
19th May 1963	Nürburgring 1000 kms	7	John Wagstaff Gil Baird	40	9th
19th May 1963	Nürburgring 1000 kms	6	Trevor Taylor David Hobbs	–	Did not finish
19th May 1963	Nürburgring 1000 kms	10	Gordon Jones Roger Nathan	–	Did not finish
15th-16th June 1963	Le Mans 24 Hrs	39	J. Pat Fergusson John Wagstaff	270	10th
15th-16th June 1963	Le Mans 24 Hrs	38	Frank Gardner John Coundley	167	Did not finish
24th August 1963	Tourist Trophy	22	Mike Beckwith Bob Olthoff	116	11th
24th August 1963	Tourist Trophy	33	Mike Johnson Robert Duggan	114	13th
24th August 1963	Tourist Trophy	32	Tom J. Threlfall John Nicholson	113	14th
24th August 1963	Tourist Trophy	21	Clive Hunt Bob Olthoff	112	16th
24th August 1963	Tourist Trophy	23	Jon A. Derisley John Nicholson	19	Did not finish
24th August 1963	Tourist Trophy	35	Roger Nathan	14	Did not finish
25th August 1963	Swiss Mountain G.P.	73	Pierre de Siebenthal		34th
25th August 1963	Swiss Mountain G.P.	60	Lionel W. Goei		60th
25th August 1963	Swiss Mountain G.P.	67	Arnaldo Maestrini		61st
8th September 1963	Monza Coppa Inter-Europa	21	Pierre de Siebenthal	83	4th

LOTUS ELITE RACING RECORD

DATE	EVENT	CAR NO.	DRIVERS	LAPS COMPLETED	RACE RESULT
16th February 1964	Daytona 2000 kms	98	Alan Bouverat Milo Vega	245	16th
21st-22ndth June 1964	Le Mans 24 Hrs	43	Clive Hunt John Wagstaff	266	22nd
9th August 1964	Freiburg-Schauinsland Hillclimb	18	"James Bond"		31st
30th August 1963	Swiss Mountain G.P.	110	Arnaldo Maestrini		53rd
29th August 1965	Swiss Mountain G.P.	78	Michel Linder		42nd
29th August 1965	Swiss Mountain G.P.	79	Arnaldo Maestrini		Did not finish
5th June 1966	Nürburgring 1000 kms	111	Arno Gyltman Ragnar Eklund	31	37th
5th June 1966	Nürburgring 1000 kms	114	Friedhelm Theissen Rolf Stommelen	7	Did not finish

TYPE 15

The Lotus 15 was a 1.5-litre Sports racing car and with a 2-litre or 2.2-litre Coventry Climax engine competed in 3-litre (Sports Car Manufacturer's Championship) events.

The multi-tubular frame follows established Lotus practice, comprising 1 inch and 0.75 inch square and round tubing, with the material thickness varying between 18 (0.048in) and 20 (0.036in) s.w.g. Frame stiffness is enhanced by the propeller-shaft tunnel and floor, which are stressed members forming an integral part of the frame.

Probably the most interesting design feature of the Lotus Fifteen is the fitting of the Coventry Climax "twin-cam" engine at an angle of some 60 degrees from the vertical. This layout has the advantage of reducing bonnet height and therefore front area. Height at the top of the scuttle is exactly two feet.

One of the Lotus Fifteen's most memorable performances was in 1958 at the British Grand Prix when Roy Salvadori drove John Coombs' private 2-litre Lotus Fifteen into second place. This was in the Sports Car Race.

Peter Heath won the 1961 8th Macau Grand Prix in a Lotus 15. This was in chassis number 620 and won in a time of 3 hours 29 minutes 30.8 seconds.

LOTUS TYPE 15 SPECIFICATIONS

FRAME:
Multi-tubular space frame. The engine is carried on two rubber mountings at the front and a single rubber mounting at the rear attached tot he bell housing; it is tilted sideways through approximately 60 degrees. The rear frame incorporates a spare wheel mounting and an easily detachable petrol tank to provide ready access to the final drive unit.

POWER UNIT:
Coventry Climax F.P.F. twin overhead camshaft, four cylinder engine.
Bore 81.2 mm (3.20 inches),
Stroke 71.1 mm (2.80 inches),
Capacity 1475 cc,
Maximum power output at 7200 rpm is 150 bhp. Notable features of the engine include aluminum alloy cylinder block and crankcase, wet cylinder liners, fully counterweighted crankshaft running in five 2.5 inch (63.5 mm diameter indium plated lead bronze steel back precision bearings light alloy pistons with Dyks pattern compression rings are used. There is one inlet and one exhaust valve per cylinder, these being inclined at an included angle of 66 degrees.

TRANSMISSION:
Special five-speed close ratio gearbox in unit with final drive.

DIMENSIONS:
Wheelbase	7ft 4 inches
Front track	3ft 11 inches
Rear track	4ft
Overall length	11ft 5 inches
Overall width	5ft
Height to top of scuttle	2ft
Ground clearance	5.5 inches

LOTUS 15 RACING RECORD

DATE	EVENT	DRIVERS	RACE RESULT
1st June 1958	Nürburgring 1000 kms	William Frost / N.Roberts Hicks	Did not finish
21st-22nd June 1958	Le Mans 24 Hrs	Jay Chamberlain / Pete Lovely	Did not finish
13 September 1958	Tourist Trophy (GB)	Cliff Allison / Graham Hill	Did not finish
21st March 1959	Sebring 12 Hrs	William Entwistle / Robert Hanna	Did not finish
7th June 1959	Nürburgring 1000 kms	Reg Parnell / Dave Buxton	Did not finish
21st-22nd June 1959	Le Mans 24 Hrs	Graham Hill / Derek Jolly	Did not finish
5th September 1959	Tourist Trophy (GB)	Graham Hill / Alan Stacey	Did not finish
22nd May 1960	Nürburgring 1000 kms	Douglas Graham / Keith Greene	18th
22nd May 1960	Nürburgring 1000 kms	Mike Taylor / Christopher Martyn	27th
28th May 1961	Nürburgring 1000 kms	Douglas Graham / Christopher Martyn	Not running at finish

Colin Chapman's Lotus 16 made its first appearance at Reims during the summer of 1958.

The original frames were constructed from 20-gauge tube with some 18-gauge in high-stress areas. Williams and Pritchard made the Costin bodyshells in the lightest 22-gauge aluminium but this could be easily damaged.

The front suspension was a Lotus wishbone system with the single link and anti-rollbar arrangement at the top. The rear strut layout was modified with the longer radius-rods, which were oval-section at the chassis-end and were welded into 1.5 inch 10 gauge tube picking up on the bottom chassis rails.

The cars used a 2-litre Coventry Climax F.P.F. engine, or for Formula 2 events a 1.5 Coventry Climax F.P.F. engine. Prototype Lotus 16's had the Formula 2 engine lying at 17° to the left, angled across the chassis centreline at 6 0.5° right - front to the left - rear. Chassis numbers for the Lotus 16 were 362, 362(2), 363, 364, 365, 366, 367, 368 and "B1".

In the Lotus 16's of 1959 Len Terry's perforated "stress panel" bulkhead appeared. This had the effect of stiffening the chassis and cockpit area. On those cars the front brake callipers were behind the axle.

For the 1959 season, Colin Chapman had the engine canted 17° and offset 10 0.5°.

During 1958 the Lotus 16 appeared only at the German Grand Prix and the Kentish 100 race. Cracked chassis and gearbox problems plagued the Lotus 16 and led to Graham Hill moving to B.R.M.

LOTUS TYPE 16 SPECIFICATIONS

ENGINE:
Coventry Climax FPF

GEARBOX:
Lotus 5-speed

CHASSIS:
Multi-tubular space-frame

DIMENSIONS:

Wheelbase	7ft 4 inches
Front track	47 inches
Rear track	47 inches
Weight	1080 lb

COVENTRY CLIMAX FPF DOUBLE-OVERHEAD-CAMSHAFT ENGINE:

Bore	3.2 inches
Stroke	2.8 inches
Compression ratio	10 to 1
Maximum output	141 bhp at 7000 rpm
Maximum torque	108.5 lb ft at 6500 rpm

The Lotus type 17 was supposed to be a lower and faster successor to the Lotus Eleven but it could not beat the threat from Eric Broadley's Lolas. The new body was designed by Len Terry.

The Lotus Type 17 has the traditional multi-tube space-frame chassis but in smaller tubing than before comprising 0.625 inch and 0.75 inch tubes in lightweight 20-gauge steel. An interesting feature of this car was the front suspension, which was of strut type, with each wheel located by a wide-based lower wishbone. The floor and the rear part of the propeller shaft tunnel are stressed numbers, forming an integral part of the frame.

The Lotus 17 first appeared at Aintree and was driven by Alan Stacey.

LOTUS TYPE 17 SPECIFICATIONS

ENGINE:
Coventry Climax FWA 1098 cc
Stage III

GEARBOX:
BMC B-Series in Lotus casing

FRONT SUSPENSION:
Independent by strut type including telescopic hydraulic shock absorbers and coil springs with wishbones picking up at the bottom of the shock absorbers

REAR SUSPENSION:
Independent by Lotus strut type with coil springs and telescopic shock absorbers

MAXIMUM POWER:
84 bhp at 6800 rpm

DIMENSIONS:

Wheelbase	6ft 10 inches
Front track	3ft 6 inches
Rear track	3ft 9 inches
Overall length	11ft 11 inches
Overall width	4ft 7.5 inches
Overall height	2ft 5 inches
Ground clearance	5 inches

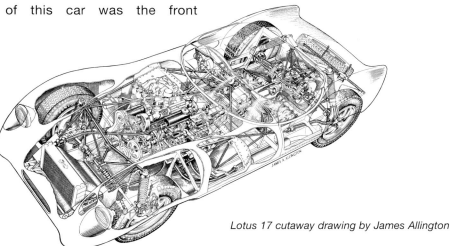

Lotus 17 cutaway drawing by James Allington

LOTUS SEVENTEEN RACING RECORD

DATE	EVENT	CAR NO.	DRIVERS	LAPS COMPLETED	RACE RESULT
7th June 1959	Nürburgring 1000 kms	29	David Piper Keith Greene	36	29th
20th-21st June 1959	Le Mans 24 Hrs	54	Mike Taylor Jonathan Sieff	23	Did not finish (Ignition)
5th September 1959	Tourist Trophy	31	Keith Greene Tony Marsh	199	11th
5th September 1959	Tourist Trophy		Innes Ireland Jay Chamberlain		Did not finish (Axle)

With the restrictions and regulations that were in force for Formula Junior, a superior performance could be obtained only by reducing power losses in the transmission and using the smallest possible frontal area. It was these two considerations which influenced Colin Chapman in utilising the rear-engine layout for his new formula junior car. This layout permits a low seating position for the driver. A front engine position would have involved either an angled propeller shaft line, or step-up gears on the in put side of the transmission if the shaft were low enough for the driver to sit above it.

The Lotus 18 uses a complete assembly from the Renault Dauphine, but it is mounted upside down. This gives two results – the input shaft is below the differential and it enables the engine to be mounted low down in the frame giving the car a very low centre of gravity.

There was insufficient rear height for the familiar strut suspension, so a new "double transverse link" arrangement was used. The transverse links located at the inner ends near the centre line of the chassis on the underside of the rear frame unit, the outer ends being attached to the bottom of the deep hub casting. Parallel radius arms ran from the engine bulkhead. The upper to just above the drive shaft and the lower to the bottom of the hub casting.

The space-type frame follows the usual tradition, but, significantly, thicker gauge tubes are used. The main structural tubes are 1 inch in diameter, of either 16 or 18 s.w.g. At the centre section, the main side tubes are spaced 2ft 0 inch apart.

Tubular wishbones are used for the front suspension. They are joined to standard Alford and Alder vertical links with upper ball joint swivels and lower screw-thread trunnions.

The rear-engine layout has dictated a change from normal Lotus practice for the rear suspension. Chapman strut-type suspension is no longer feasible.

A 22-gallon fuel tank was positioned over the drivers legs with another 9.5 gallon tank to the right of, and behind, the seat. Fuel-load was well within the wheelbase like this and minimised handling changes from full fuel to little fuel on board. The car had a weight distribution of 44% / 56% front to rear.

The Lotus 18 was extremely successful in competition. At Oulton Park in 1960 the only event not won by Lotus was the marque race in which Lotuses were not eligible to compete. In the Oulton Park Trophy Race for Formula Two cars Innes Ireland won in his Lotus 18. He won in a time of 45 minutes 27.40 seconds, and set the record for fastest lap.

First three places in the Formula Junior race were taken by the Lotuses of J.Clark (1st), T. Taylor (2nd) and M. McKee (3rd).

In the sports car race the winner was the Lotus Climax of T. Dickson. In the closed car race the Lotus Elite of C. Summers was the winner.

At the Monaco Grand Prix of 1960 Stirling Moss was victorious in a Lotus 18 in a time of 2 hours 53 minutes 45.50 seconds. This was in chassis '376'.

The following year at the 1961 Monaco Grand Prix Stirling Moss again won in a Lotus 18 in an even better time of 2 hours 45 minutes 50.10 seconds, despite the opposition from Ferrari. In 1960 Stirling Moss ran in a Lotus 18 with number 28 on it and in 1961 he ran in a Lotus 18 with number 20 on it. Also at Monaco in 1960 Trevor Taylor became British Junior champion in a Lotus 18.

Jim Clark came first at the 1961 Pau Grand Prix in chassis '371' and sixth in the Syracuse Grand Prix in chassis '374'.

At the Monaco Grand Prix of 1961 Stirling Moss came first in chassis 912, while Jim Clark came second in chassis 371 at the 1961 Guards Trophy Intercontinental.

LOTUS TYPE 18 SPECIFICATIONS

ENGINE:
Ford Anglia 105E or Coventry Climax FPF

CUBIC CAPACITY:
997 cc or 2495 cc

TRANSMISSION:
Clutch-single dry plate

GEARBOX:
Renault

FINAL DRIVE:
Spiral bevel, ratio 4.37 to 1

BRAKES:
Lockheed hydraulic (Alfin drums)

FRONT SUSPENSION:
Independent wishbone, coil spring-damper units, anti-roll bar

REAR SUSPENSION:
Independent, double wishbones, coil spring-damper units

DIMENSIONS:

Wheelbase	7ft 6 inches
Overall length	11ft 1 inch
Overall width	4ft 8.5 inches
Overall height	2ft 10.5 inches
Ground clearance	4 inches
Weight	980 lbs

LOTUS EIGHTEEN IN COMPETITION IN 1960

DATE	EVENT	DRIVERS	CHASSIS NO	RACE RESULT
7th February 1960	Argentine G.P.	Innes Ireland	369	6th
14th May 1960	B.R.D.C. Int. Trophy	Innes Ireland	371	1st
14th May 1960	B.R.D.C. Int. Trophy	Alan Stacey	370	4th
29th May 1960	Monaco Grand Prix	Stirling Moss	376	1st
6th June 1960	Dutch Grand Prix	Innes Ireland	371	2nd
16th June 1960	British Grand Prix	John Surtees	373	2nd
19th June 1960	Belgian Grand Prix	Jim Clark	373	5th
14th August 1960	Portuguese Grand Prix	Jim Clark	374	3rd
17th September 1960	Lombank Trophy	Innes Ireland	372	1st
17th September 1960	Lombank Trophy	Jim Clark	374	2nd
29th September 1960	Gold Cup, Oulton Park	Stirling Moss	376	1st
9th October 1960	Watkins Glen	Stirling Moss	376	1st
20th November 1960	United States G.P.	Stirling Moss	376	1st
20th November 1960	United States G.P.	Innes Ireland	372	2nd

Lotus 18 CHASSIS NUMBERS

Chassis numbers of Lotus Eighteens were 369, 370, 371, 372, 373, 374, 375, 376, 900, 901, 902, 903, 904, 905, 906, 907, 908, 909, 910, 911, 912, 913, 914, 915, 916 and 917.

Innes Ireland driving the Lotus Nineteen at Snetterton on 30th March 1963

The Lotus 19 was also called the Lotus Monte Carlo in recognition of Lotus winning their first Grand Prix at Monaco in May 1960. This was by Stirling Moss in Rob Walker's Lotus 18.

The Lotus Monte Carlo is virtually a copy of the Lotus 18, but the space frame chassis has been widened out.

An unusual feature on the Lotus is the location of the front coil spring/damper units on tubes in bending. To compensate for the extra loading involved, the short tube between the two wishbone mountings is of 1.125 inch, 14-gauge mild steel, as against the 1inch and 0.75 inch 16 and 18-gauge tubing used for the rest of the chassis.

Stirling Moss tested the first Lotus 19 car and it was driven to victory by him at Karlskoga, Sweden on the 7th August 1960 in a time of 41' 08.8". The following morning Joakim Bonnier used the Lotus 19 to set up a new Swedish speed record for the flying kilometre at a speed of 252.3 kph. (157.5 mph).

Dan Gurney gained first place at Daytona 3 Hrs on 11th of February 1962 after completing 82 laps, while John Coundley gained seventh place at the Tourist Trophy on the 29th August 1964 after completing 125 laps.

LOTUS 19 SPECIFICATIONS

ENGINE:
Climax FPF 2495 cc

CHASSIS:
Multi-tubular space-frame

BODY:
Aluminium underpan and rockers

DIMENSIONS:

Height	31 inches
Width	60.5 inches
Length	139.25 inches
Curb weight	1240 lbs
Front track	51 inches
Rear track	50 inches

The Lotus Twenty was a Ford-powered projectile, out to emulate its predecessor as the most successful car in its class. Colin Chapman and his design associates did their customary wonderful job and improved the road-holding, increased the streamlining and reduced the frontal area. The centre of gravity was lowered further by the use of a more reclining driver's seat, dropped engine mountings, and a re-sited fuel tank. Fuel on the 1960 model was carried in a tank over the driver's legs, and in another beside the seat.

The new car has a lightweight eight-gallon tank mounted aft and slightly underneath the driver's backrest.

It is a fact that with the exception of the drive-shafts nothing on the new car is interchangeable with the old. Probably the single greatest effect on the height of the car is the switch from 15 inch to 13 inch wheels at the front.

Trevor Taylor and Peter Arundell enjoyed great success with the car, and the Prix Monaco Junior of 1961 was won by Peter Arundell in a Lotus 20.

LOTUS 20 SPECIFICATIONS

ENGINE:
Ford 105E

GEARBOX:
Renault 4-speed or VW Gearbox

CHASSIS:
Multi-tubular space-frame

DIMENSIONS:

Wheelbase	7ft 6 inches
Front track	4ft 1 inch
Rear track	4ft
Ground clearance	3.75inches

PRICE:

Kit form	£1450
Assembled for export	£1525

The Lotus Type 21 is based on a space-frame chassis, and had four main bulkheads and complete triangulation of all bays except the one occupied by the driver's body. Both frontal cross-section and overall height are much reduced by comparison with the Lotus Type 18.

The rear suspension is based on the principle of taking loads out over the widest possible base, thereby reducing the stresses involved to a minimum.

Chassis numbers for the Lotus 21 were 930, 931, 932, 933, 934, 935, 936, 937, 938, 939 and 952.

The power unit is the 4-cylinder Coventry Climax FPF Mark II, inclined 20° to the right to reduce its overall height. It is mounted immediately behind the seat-back bulkhead and bolted direct to an entirely new 5-speed gearbox made by German firm ZF. Because of confusion over the gearbox Innes Ireland crashed his car. Innes Ireland scored the first championship win at the United States Grand Prix in October 1961 with the Lotus 21, and this car was chassis number '933'.

Jim Clark came first in the Rand GP of 1961 and the Natal GP of 1961 (South Africa) in chassis 937. He also won the South African Grand Prix, East London in December 1961. Trevor Taylor won the Cape G.P. in 1962 with chassis 933.

LOTUS TYPE 21 SPECIFICATIONS

ENGINE:
Coventry Climax FPF Mark II

GEARBOX:
ZF Five-speed

CUBIC CAPACITY:
1495 cc

CHASSIS:
Multi-tubular space-frame

FRONT SUSPENSION:
Fabricated upper wishbone acting on coil/damper unit

REAR SUSPENSION:
Reversed lower wishbones, two transverse links, outboard coil spring/damper units

DIMENSIONS:
Wheelbase	7ft 6 inches
Overall length	4ft 5.5 inches

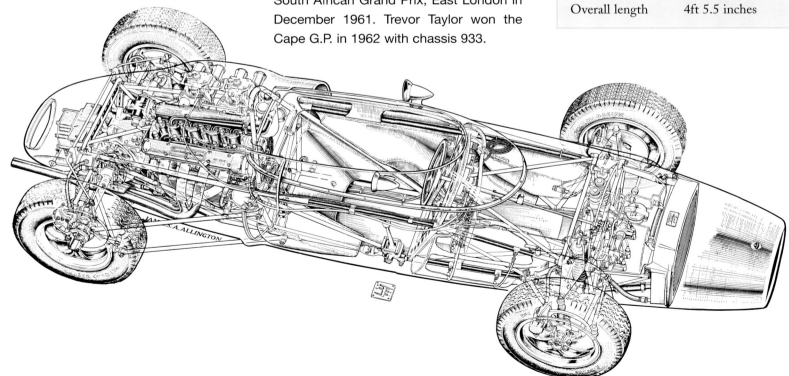

The Lotus Type 22 was a logical development of the works Lotus 20 and the most important alteration was the use of the Cosworth-Ford 1100 cc engine for all Lotus Formula Juniors. As far as Lotus were concerned the 997 cc Junior version of the Ford 105E engine had passed into history.

The "1100" had to carry an extra weight penalty, and that weight was built into the car rather than being found by ballast. Peter Arundell, a Team Lotus Driver, won 18 out of 25 races in 1962. He was Lotus's number one Junior man in the 1962 season. He demonstrated the ability of the Lotus 22 when he put in two consecutive laps of Goodwood in under 1 minute 30 seconds.

Jo Siffert was thirteenth in the first heat of the 1962 Brussels G.P. with chassis 22-J-7. Bob van Niekerk was fourteenth in the 1962 Rand GP with chassis 22-J-37 and came sixth in the second heat of the 1962 Natal G.P in the same car.

The Lotus 22 was first shown at the Racing Car Show in January 1962. Cost in component form was £1550.

LOTUS TYPE 22 SPECIFICATIONS

ENGINE:
Cosworth-Ford 1100 cc O.H.V.

GEARBOX:
Renault 4-speed or VW 4-speed

CHASSIS:
Multi-tubular space-frame

BRAKES:
Girling disc brakes outboard front and rear

POWER:
100 bhp at 7500 rpm

FUEL SYSTEM:
Light alloy fuel tank with roughly an 8-gallon capacity

FRONT SUSPENSION:
Double wishbones of unequal length and coil spring/damper units

REAR SUSPENSION:
Reversed lower wishbones, single transverse top link and coil spring/damper units

DIMENSIONS:

Wheelbase	7ft 6 inches
Front track	4ft 3.5 inches
Rear track	4ft 2 inches
Length	11ft 7 inches
Height to crash bar	2ft 8 inches
Ground clearance	3.75 inches

WHEELS AND TYRES:
Lightweight cast magnesium wheels 13 inches diameter at front and rear.

TYPE 23 AND 23B

The Lotus Type 23 was based on the all-conquering Lotus 22 Formula Junior car of 1961. The specification included an 1100 cc 103 bhp Cosworth-Ford engine that was mounted behind the driver in a space-frame chassis.

The top-left and bottom-right longitudinal chassis members are used as water pipes linking engine and radiator, whilst the top-right and bottom-left members act as oil pipes.

The bodywork of resin-bonded glass-fibre was designed to comply with Appendix J Group IV Sports Car regulations of 1962 in respect of windscreen height, luggage space, ground clearance and turning circle.

The Lotus 23 made its first appearance at the Nürburgring 1000 km race of 1962. At this race Jim Clark had dominated an opposition comprised of Ferrari's, Porsche and Aston Martin before crashing off the track with a damaged exhaust.

Two Lotus 23's were entered for Le Mans but the cars were refused entry on the grounds that the front wheels had a four-stud fixing whereas the rear wheels had a six-stud fixing. Colin Chapman altered the cars to take the four-stud wheels at the back but the Lotus 23s were again refused entry. Colin Chapman never raced again at Le Mans.

From 1963, a Lotus 23B was available with a strengthened chassis and a Hewland five-speed gearbox and final drive. It came with a Lotus-Ford twin-cam 1594 cc engine.

Ian Geoghegan won the Australian TT in a Lotus 23, and many other successes awaited the car. Alan Rees and Peter Arundell achieved second place at the Auvergne Trophy on 15th July 1962 after completing 38 laps. The following year at the same race Tony Hegbourne achieved second place with a Lotus 23B, and Mike Beckwith achieved fifth place with his Lotus 23B.

Anton Fischhaber and Karl Foitek regularly used the Lotus 23 in hill climb events. At Freiburg-Schauinsland hill climb events on the 11th August 1963 Anton Fischhaber achieved sixth place in a Lotus BWW 23, while Karl Foitek achieved seventeenth place in the Sports Prototype Group. Just two weeks later in the Swiss Mountain Grand Prix Karl Foitek was sixth and Anton Fischhaber was eighth.

After the Nürburgring 1000 Kms on 1st September 1963 Fritz Baumann gained second place in the Prototype GT Group while Dick Young and George Alderman gained second place in the Bridgehampton Double 500 on the 18th September 1965.

LOTUS TYPE 23 SPECIFICATIONS

ENGINE:
Cosworth-Ford 1100 cc O.H.V. four cylinder with two 40 DCOE Weber Carburettors

TRANSMISSION:
Renault or Volkswagen modified close ratio four-speed gearbox

CHASSIS:
Multi-tubular space frame constructed of round, square and rectangular section tubing

FRONT SUSPENSION:
Fully independent by double wishbone type, incorporating parallel radius rods and also a top link

DIMENSIONS:

Wheelbase	90 inches
Front track	51.5 inches
Rear track	50 inches
Overall length	140 inches
Overall width	59.5 inches
Overall height	27 inches
Ground clearance	3.75 inches

Cosworth-Ford 1097 cc giving 96 bhp at 7600 rpm
Cosworth-Ford Mark XI giving 100 bhp at 7800 rpm
Lotus-Ford 1600 cc twin-cam giving 140 bhp at 6500 rpm

At the Nürburgring 1000 km Jim Clark had shocked Ferrari by taking the lead with the Lotus-Ford 23

LOTUS 23 AND 23B

PRODUCTION:
April 1962 to May 1966

BUILT:
131 cars

LOTUS 23 RACING RECORD

DATE	EVENT	CAR NO.	DRIVERS	LAPS COMPLETED	RACE RESULT
27th May 1962	Nürburgring 1000 kms	65	Peter Ashdown Bruce Johnston	40	8th
27th May 1962	Nürburgring 1000 kms	64	Paul Hawkins Peter Ryan	26	Did not finish (Overheating)
27th May 1962	Nürburgring 1000 kms	84	Jim Clark Trevor Taylor	11	Did not finish
15th July 1962	Auvergne Trophy	18	Alan Rees Peter Arundell	38	2nd
15th July 1962	Auvergne Trophy	44	Bernard Consten	36	9th
15th July 1962	Auvergne Trophy	24	Paul Hawkins	32	22nd
21st October 1962	Paris 1000 Kms	42	Jose Rosinski Bernard Consten	112	11th
2nd June 1963	Consuma Hillclimb	42	Cesare Toppetti		6th
9th June 1963	Rossfeld Hillclimb	25	Anton Fischhaber		43rd
9th June 1963	Rossfeld Hillclimb	15	Walter Schatz		69th
9th June 1963	Rossfeld Hillclimb	14	Kurt Rost Fritz Baumann		79th
7th July 1963	Auvergne Trophy	6	Tony Hegbourne	46	2nd
7th July 1963	Auvergne Trophy	8	Mike Beckwith	44	5th
11th August 1963	Freiburg-Schauinsland Hillclimb	71	Anton Fischhaber		6th
11th August 1963	Freiburg-Schauinsland Hillclimb	61	Kurt Rost		8th
11th August 1963	Freiburg-Schauinsland Hillclimb	62	Robert Huber		9th
11th August 1963	Freiburg-Schauinsland Hillclimb	63	Karl Foitek		17th
11th August 1963	Freiburg-Schauinsland Hillclimb	56	Fritz Baumann		22nd

LOTUS 23 RACING RECORD

DATE	EVENT	CAR NO.	DRIVERS	LAPS COMPLETED	RACE RESULT
11th August 1963	Freiburg-Schauinsland Hillclimb	54	Walter Schatz		25th
11th August 1963	Freiburg-Schauinsland Hillclimb	59	Alban Scheiber		Did not finish
25th August 1963	Swiss Mountain G.P.	139	Karl Foitek		6th
25th August 1963	Swiss Mountain G.P.	154	Anton Fischhaber		8th
25th August 1963	Swiss Mountain G.P.	140	Robert Huber		9th
25th August 1963	Swiss Mountain G.P.	141	Kurt Rost		11th
25th August 1963	Swiss Mountain G.P.	121	Fritz Baumann		21st
25th August 1963	Swiss Mountain G.P.	131	Bernhard Baur		22nd
25th August 1963	Swiss Mountain G.P.	128	Walter Schatz		30th
25th August 1963	Swiss Mountain G.P.	142	Alban Scheiber		Did not finish
1st September 1963	Nürburgring 1000 Kms	86	Fritz Baumann	22	2nd
26th May 1964	Consuma Hillclimb	340	Cesare Toppetti		5th
7th June 1964	Rossfeld Mountain G.P.	7	Karl Foitek		4th
7th June 1964	Rossfeld Mountain G.P.	8	Peter Westbury		5th
7th June 1964	Rossfeld Mountain G.P.	4	Anton Fischhaber		10th
7th June 1964	Rossfeld Mountain G.P.	15	Walter Schatz		18th
9th August 1964	Freiburg-Schauinsland Hillclimb	103	Karl Foitek		11th
9th August 1964	Freiburg-Schauinsland Hillclimb	95	Anton Fischhaber		13th
9th August 1964	Freiburg-Schauinsland Hillclimb	104	Robert Huber		15th
9th August 1964	Freiburg-Schauinsland Hillclimb	88	Walter Schatz		19th

LOTUS 23 RACING RECORD

DATE	EVENT	CAR NO.	DRIVERS	LAPS COMPLETED	RACE RESULT
29th August 1964	Tourist Trophy	6	David Hobbs Richard Attwood	77	Did not finish (Clutch)
30th August 1964	Swiss Mountain G.P.	64	Anton Fischhaber		11th
30th August 1964	Swiss Mountain G.P.	55	Karl Foitek		13th
30th August 1964	Swiss Mountain G.P.	43	Walter Schatz		18th
30th August 1964	Swiss Mountain G.P.	41	Emil Knecht		44th
30th August 1964	Swiss Mountain G.P.	65	David Good		Did not finish
1st May 1965	Tourist Trophy	8	Chris Williams	81	Did not finish
6th June 1965	Circuit of Mugello	43	Massimo Natili "Terry"	7	17th
6th June 1965	Circuit of Mugello	46	Bruno Momigliano Remigio Cianfriglia	7	20th
13th June 1965	Rossfeld Hillclimb	7	Walter Schatz		14th
13th June 1965	Rossfeld Hillclimb	15	Heini Buess		28th
8th August 1965	Freiburg-Schauinsland	53	Robert Huber		14th
8th August 1965	Freiburg-Schauinsland	63	Anton Fischhaber		16th
8th August 1965	Freiburg-Schauinsland	49	Heini Buess		22nd
29th August 1965	Swiss Mountain G.P.	165	Alban Scheiber		9th
29th August 1965	Swiss Mountain G.P.	173	Walter Schatz		11th
29th August 1965	Swiss Mountain G.P.	163	Pierre Marx		34th
29th August 1965	Swiss Mountain G.P.	150	Heini Buess		35th
18th September 1965	Bridgehampton Double 500	25	Dick Young George Alderman		2nd
18th September 1965	Bridgehampton Double 500	42	Candida DaMota		12th
19th September 1965	Bridgehampton Double 500	16	Skip Barber		Did not finish

LOTUS 23 RACING RECORD

DATE	EVENT	CAR NO.	DRIVERS	LAPS COMPLETED	RACE RESULT
5th June 1966	Nürburgring 1000 kms	28	Rico Steinemann Andreas Eichhorn		Did not finish
17th July 1966	Circuit of Mugello	165	Secondo Ridolfi Bruno Momigliano	6	Not classified
14th August 1966	Hockenheim G.P.	4	Anton Fischhaber	67	7th
28th August 1966	Swiss Mountain G.P.	36	Xavier Perrot		9th
28th August 1966	Swiss Mountain G.P.	194	Eric Feldmann		18th
28th August 1966	Swiss Mountain G.P.	180	Bruno Frey		35th
23rd July 1967	Circuit of Mugello	38	J.Peter de Meritt Jean Blanc	3	Did not finish
27th August 1967	Swiss Mountain G.P.	203	Henri Buergisser		32nd
27th August 1967	Swiss Mountain G.P.	51	Xavier Perrot		Did not finish

Note the different positioning of the gearshift lever on these two Lotus 23B's

The Lotus Type 24 was originally meant to appear in 1961, but delays in production of its Coventry Climax engine meant that the prototype was not completed until March 1962. The Lotus 24 made its debut on 1 April 1962 at the Brussels Grand Prix where it had recorded fastest practice time but retired on the opening lap with a broken tappet.

The Lotus 24 resembled the Lotus 21 but was designed to take the new Coventry Climax FWMV V8 engine. Arch motors built the space frame chassis and they had replaced Progress Chassis Company as Lotus chassis builders.

The Coventry Climax engine was of straight forward design with the cylinder banks separated at 90°. Running at 8500 rpm the V-8 Climax needs 567 sparks per second and this is provided by the Lucas transistors.

Trevor Taylor's second place in a Lotus 24 at the Dutch Grand Prix was probably one of its best results, but the Lotus 24 was quickly replaced by the Lotus 25.

Jim Clark won the Aintree 200 on 28th April 1962 in a Lotus 24 and Snetterton on 14th April 1962

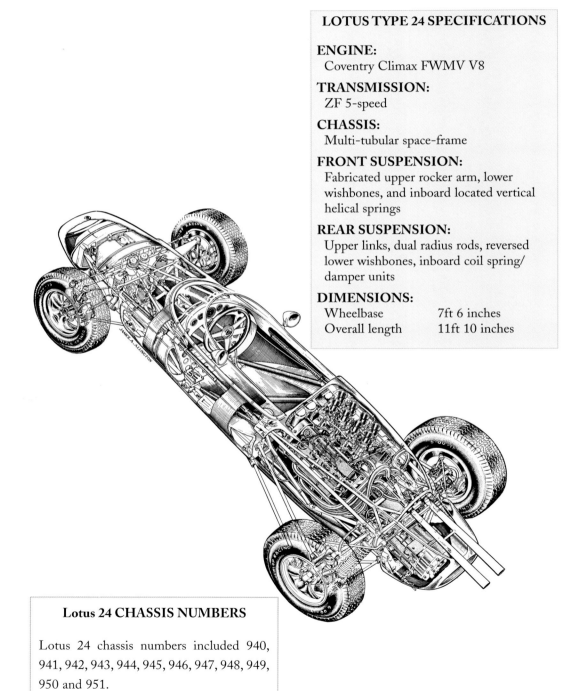

LOTUS TYPE 24 SPECIFICATIONS

ENGINE:
Coventry Climax FWMV V8

TRANSMISSION:
ZF 5-speed

CHASSIS:
Multi-tubular space-frame

FRONT SUSPENSION:
Fabricated upper rocker arm, lower wishbones, and inboard located vertical helical springs

REAR SUSPENSION:
Upper links, dual radius rods, reversed lower wishbones, inboard coil spring/damper units

DIMENSIONS:
Wheelbase	7ft 6 inches
Overall length	11ft 10 inches

Lotus 24 CHASSIS NUMBERS

Lotus 24 chassis numbers included 940, 941, 942, 943, 944, 945, 946, 947, 948, 949, 950 and 951.

The Lotus Type 25 was revolutionary in Formula 1 and was the first car to feature a monocoque or "twin-tube ladder-frame" chassis.

This car had more torsional stiffness, and therefore more cornering power, than the conventional multi-tubular chassis. It also weighed about twenty pounds less than the chassis and body of the Lotus 24. Fuel is carried in rubber bags hung inside the chassis/body side members. They have a total capacity of 26 gallons.

The Lotus 25's chassis was based on two longitudinal aluminium torsion-boxes that ran either side of the cockpit. Front and rear bulkheads carried the wishbone suspension. Whilst Colin Chapman had done the original layout and exterior design for the Lotus 25 much of the detail work was carried out by chief draughtsman Alan Styman.

Jim Clark won at the Belgian Grand Prix at Spa and set a new record at 133.57 mph.

LOTUS 25 SPECIFICATIONS

ENGINE:
Climax FWMV 90º V8

CAPACITY:
1497 cc

GEARBOX:
ZF 5D510 five-speed

CHASSIS:
Aluminium monocoque, steel-cross members

Jim Endruweit and Dick Scammell with the Lotus 25 that Trevor Taylor drove to 12th place in the 1962 United States Grand Prix at Watkins Glen

Jim Clark achieved great corner-speeds with Lotus 25, seen here on the Indy pit lane

Successes of the Lotus 25

Jim Clark	Lotus 25	Chassis R1	1st	Belgian Grand Prix	17th	June 1962
Jim Clark	Lotus 25	Chassis R2	1st	British Grand Prix	21st	July 1962
Jim Clark	Lotus 25	Chassis R2	1st	Oulton Park Gold Cup	1st	September 1962
Jim Clark	Lotus 25	Chassis R2	1st	Mexican Grand Prix	4th	November 1962
Trevor Taylor	Lotus 25	Chassis R2	1st	Natal Grand Prix	22nd	December 1962
Jim Clark	Lotus 25	Chassis R3	1st	U.S.A. Grand Prix	7th	October 1962
Jim Clark	Lotus 25	Chassis R3	1st	Kanonlopet, Karlskoga	11th	August 1962

TYPE 25

Another view of the Lotus 25 at the Indianapolis track.

Successes of the Lotus 25

Jim Clark	Lotus 25	Chassis R4	1st	Belgian Grand Prix	9th	June 1963
Jim Clark	Lotus 25	Chassis R4	1st	Dutch Grand Prix	23rd	June 1963
Jim Clark	Lotus 25	Chassis R4	1st	French Grand Prix	30th	June 1963
Jim Clark	Lotus 25	Chassis R4	1st	British Grand Prix	20th	July 1963
Jim Clark	Lotus 25	Chassis R4	1st	Italian Grand Prix	8th	September 1963
Jim Clark	Lotus 25	Chassis R4	1st	Oulton Park Gold Cup	21st	September 1963
Jim Clark	Lotus 25	Chassis R4	1st	Mexican Grand Prix	27th	October 1963
Jim Clark	Lotus 25	Chassis R4	1st	South African Grand Prix	28th	December 1963
Jim Clark	Lotus 25	Chassis R5	1st	Pau Grand Prix	15th	April 1963
Jim Clark	Lotus 25	Chassis R5	1st	Imola Grand Prix	21st	April 1963
Jim Clark	Lotus 25	Chassis R5	1st	International Trophy Silverstone	11th	May 1963

The "bathtub" - chassied stressed - skin car's Coventry Climax V8 engine

Successes of the Lotus 25

Jim Clark	Lotus 25	Chassis R6	1st	Goodwood	30th March 1964
Jim Clark	Lotus 25	Chassis R6	1st	Dutch Grand Prix	24th May 1964
Jim Clark	Lotus 25	Chassis R6	1st	Belgian Grand Prix	14th June 1964
Jim Clark	Lotus 25	Chassis R6	1st	British Grand Prix	11th July 1964
Jim Clark	Lotus 25	Chassis R6	1st	Goodwood International	19th April 1965
Jim Clark	Lotus 25	Chassis R6	1st	French Grand Prix	27th June 1965

LOTUS ELAN S2 SPECIFICATIONS

ENGINE:
Four stroke. Four cylinders in line, cast iron block

CUBIC CAPACITY:
1558 cc

BORE AND STROKE:
82.55 mm bore

MAXIMUM OUTPUT:
105 bhp at 5500 rpm

COMPRESSION RATIO:
9.5 to 1

TRANSMISSION:
Single-dry-plate clutch. Four-speed all-synchromesh gearbox with floor-mounted shift.

FRONT SUSPENSION:
Independent with unequal length wishbones, coil springs and telescopic dampers

Wheelbase	84 inches
Front track	46.2 inches
Rear track	48.0 inches
Length	145.2 inches
Width	56.0 inches

The Lotus project that developed into what we now know as the Lotus Elan was named Project M2.

Colin Chapman wanted an engine for the car and approached Harry Munday who had been technical editor of the Autocar magazine. Colin Chapman wanted a twin-cam unit and Harry Munday designed this to fit the 105E block. All the development of this engine was done at Lotus by Steve Sanville and his team, while glassfibre work on the original Lotus Elan was done by Albert Adams.

The 105E engine was the only one of the Ford range in existence when development of the Lotus head started. As the 109E and 116E were developed the head was modified to fit the slightly different blocks.

The Lotus Elan S2 became available by November 1964, and the Lotus Elan S3 became available by the autumn of 1965 with the Lotus Elan S4 being introduced in March 1968. The Lotus Elan S4 Sprint was available by 1971. Gold Leaf Sprints can be seen with gold wheel centres but they never left the factory like that. The authentic specification was either black or silver.

The Lotus Elan 26R was the competition version of the Elan and had thinner glass-fibre panels. Lotus Elan 26Rs were raced by Stirling Moss Automobile Racing Team and Team Willment. The Lotus Elan 26R won the Autosport Championship in 1966.

On the Lotus Elan 26R, Lotus saved almost 100lb by casting the Lotus Cortina gearbox housing in magnesium, along with the housing for the limited-slip differential. Fred Ashplant came third in the 1965 Bridgehampton Double with his 26R.

The Lotus Type 27 was the last Formula Junior car produced by Lotus, the first having been the Lotus 18. The Lotus 27 was a development of the Lotus 25 but was a new and very advanced Formula Junior car.

While the interior panelling is 18-gauge aluminium sheet the outer panels are of 0.25 inch glass fibre. The two materials are then pop-rivetted together. The front bulkhead was also fabricated from sheet steel as is the rear.

Of the front wishbones, the bottom ones are of tubular construction but at the top there are boxed-in members which are extended to operate the usual Lotus inboard spring and damper units. Front suspension uprights are Triumph Herald components.

For 1963 Formula Junior drivers for Lotus were Peter Arundell, Mike Spence and John Fenning. Peter Arundell won the first race of the year at Oulton Park with the Lotus 27.

LOTUS TYPE 27 SPECIFICATIONS

ENGINE:
Cosworth-Ford 1097 cc

GEARBOX:
Mark IV 5-speed Hewland, based on the Volkswagen box

CHASSIS:
Monocoque construction from 18-gauge aluminium sheet

FRONT SUSPENSION:
Upper lever arms, lower wishbones and inboard coil spring/damper units

REAR SUSPENSION:
Reversed lower wishbones, single top links, parallel radius arms, and outboard coil spring/damper units

WHEELBASE:
7ft 6 inches

MAXIMUM TRACK:
4ft 3.5 inches

OVERALL LENGTH:
11ft 7 inches

WHEELS:
Bolt-on magnesium

TYRES:
4.50 x 13 inches and 5.5 x 13 inches Dunlop for front and rear respectively

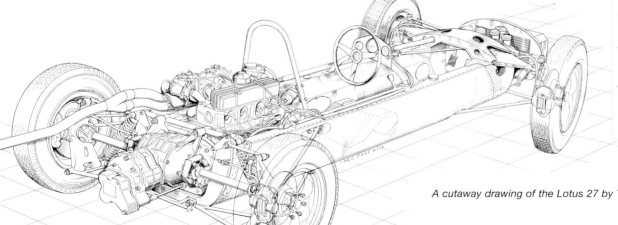

A cutaway drawing of the Lotus 27 by Theo Page

TYPE 28

The Lotus-Cortina Mark I, also know as the Consul Cortina Sports Special, was made to meet the demand for a production sports car both in Britain and abroad.

Team Lotus announced that they would be entering the car in major saloon car racing events and drivers would include Jim Clark, Trevor Taylor and Peter Arundell.

The Lotus Cortina has a 105 bhp 1558 cc twin-overhead-camshaft engine and two twin choke Weber carburettors. The Lotus Cortina develops its 105 bhp at 5500 rpm and 108 lbs/ft of torque at 4000 rpm. Though the body seemed similar to that of the family saloon it had aluminium outer panels on the doors, body and bonnet. It was identifiable by the striking green flash down the side of the white body and by the green-on-yellow Lotus crest.

In 1964 the cost of the Lotus-Cortina including purchase tax was £1100 3s 1d, nearly twice as much as the cheapest 1200 Cortina.

In June 1965 half-elliptic leaf springs and twin radius arms were introduced on the Lotus-Cortina.

In October 1965 self-adjusting rear-brakes were adopted and from 1966 Group 5 cars had Lucas fuel injection and dry sumps.

Lotus-Cortina acceleration times were:
0 – 30 mph	3.6 seconds
0 – 60 m.p.h	9.4 seconds
0 – 90 mph	23.0 seconds

LOTUS TYPE 28 SPECIFICATIONS

ENGINE:
4 cylinder, twin o.h.c., water cooled
Bore	82.55 mm
Stroke	72.746 mm
Cubic capacity	1558 cc
Compression ratio	9.5 to 1

TYRES:
6.00 x 13

GEAR RATIOS (all synchromesh):
First	2.50 to 1
Second	1.64 to 1
Third	1.23 to 1
Fourth	1 to 1
Final drive optional	3.90 to 1; 3.77 to 1;
	4.1 to 1; 4.43 to 1

DIMENSIONS:
Track	F. 51.6in; R. 49.5in
Wheelbase	98.4 in
Length	168.3 in
Width	62.5 in
Height	53.4 in
Ground clearance	5.3 in

BRAKES:
F. disc (9.75 in dia);
R. drum (1LS, 9 in x 1.75 in)

CLUTCH:
Single dry plate

FUEL SYSTEM:
Two twin-choke Weber (G-O DCOE2) carbs

FUEL CAPACITY:
8 gallon

SUSPENSION:
Front – independent through coilsprings and double acting telescopic shock absorbers; anti-roll torsion bar
Rear – coilsprings and telescopic shock absorbers. Rear axle located by radius arms and A-Frame

The above photograph shows an ex-Police car from West Sussex, registered GBP 1C (Chassis Number BA74ER59347) and now owned by Keith Halstead in Essex.

The Lotus Cortina achieved much success including 1st place in the Saloon Car Race at Snetterton on 28th September 1963 and 1st in the Saloon Car Race at Oulton Park on 11th April 1964, and 1st again at Crystal Palace on the 18th May 1964 and Oulton Park on 19th September 1964. In September 1964, Vic Elford and David Seigle-Morris gained 11th place in the Touring Group of that year's Tour de France. In 1965 it was 1st in the Three Hours Race, Sebring on the 26th March and at Goodwood on the 19th April 1965. In 1966 on 29th August at Brands Hatch it was first again in the Saloon Car Race. It was driven to success on all these occasions by Jim Clark, as it was on 17th September 1966 at Oulton Park.

The Lotus Cortina of Bengt Söderström and Gunnar Palm won the 1967 Swedish Rally and came third in the Acropolis Rally. Bengt Söderström and Gunnar Palm also gained second place in the Munich – Vienna Budapest Rally of 1967. Ove Andersson and Nordhlund gained 4th place in the Rally of 1000 Lakes in 1967.

At the Daytona 24 Hours of February 1967, Ross L. Bremmer, Don Kearney and Billy Turner gained twenty-second place in the Touring Group with car number 89.

Lotus Cortina was distinguishable from the standard Cortina by the fact that the front suspension had a stiffer stabiliser bar, shorter steering arms and changed wheel alignment settings.

Jim Clark in Lotus Mk I BJH 417B

TECHNICAL ENGINE DATA

PISTONS:

Piston clearance	0.0027 inches to 0.0033 inches
Compression ring gaps	0.009 inches to 0.014 inches
Compression ring to groove clearance	0.0016 inches to 0.0036 inches
Oil-control ring gap	0.010 inches to 0.020 inches
Oil control ring to groove clearance	0.0018 inches to 0.0038 inches

VALVES

Valve clearance when cold

Inlet	0.005 inches to 0.006 inches
Exhaust	0.006 inches to 0.007 inches

Valve timing

Inlet opens	22° b.t.d.c.
Inlet closes	62° a.b.d.c.
Exhaust opens	62° b.b.d.c.
Exhaust closes	22° a.t.d.c.
Valve-guide inside diameter	0.3113 inches to 0.3125 inches
Valve-stem diameter	0.310 inches to 0.311 inches

Valve-head diameter

Inlet	1.526 inches to 1.1530 inches
Exhaust	1.321 inches to 1.325 inches

TYPE 29

The Lotus Type 29 was based as closely as possible on the Lotus 25 with any modifications being to accommodate the different power unit and transmission, the larger volume of fuel, and the modified suspension set-up dictated by the left-hand bias of the Indy circuit.

Indy regulations lay down a minimum wheelbase of 96 inches, which makes the Lotus 29 five inches longer than the Lotus 25. The side numbers are 1.75 inches deeper and slightly wider to accommodate the bag tanks holding 50 US Gallons of fuel. The tank space is divided into six separate compartments, all interconnected to allow for pressure refuelling. Five of the six tanks are rubber aircraft type, and the sixth, above the driver's legs, is of aluminium, encased in glass fibre. All six were interconnected and refuelled under pressure through a Demon inlet valve on the hull's left side. Non return valves between the tanks prevented fuel surge from left to right through the anti-clockwise turns. They opened to allow rear-ward flow into the collectors under acceleration.

Ford of America were used to supply the engines of the Indy Lotuses. They are based on the 4260 cc V8 Fairlane unit, and had aluminium heads and block, dry-sump lubrication, four 58 mm twin-choke Weber carburettors and an output of around 402 horsepower at 7000 rpm.

Transmission is by a Colotti-Francis Type 37A gearbox-final-drive unit, but only two gears were used in the race.

The chassis is offset 2.375 inches to the left from the centre line of the track. This has been achieved at the front by making the right-side suspensions links longer than those on the left. At the rear the links are the same length, but the pick-up points are offset the required amount.

The Lotus 29 Prototype with symmetrical suspension was tested at Snetterton in March 1963 before being flown to the USA and the Ford's Kingman, Arizona test track. It lapped at 165 mph but the V8 engine was unreliable. The Lotus Prototype (Chassis 29/1) was also known as "The Mule" and it was in this car that Dan Gurney came 7th when the car had number 93 on it. Gurney also came 3rd in the Milwaukee 200 in August 1963 whilst retiring from the Trenton 200 in September 1963. As well as the three cars chassis 29/1, 29/2 and 29/3 it is believed there were a trio of some Type 29 replicas assembled by Carroll Horton around new-made chassis tubs. Team Lotus had supplied Type 29 components to American owners during the 1960's and it was therefore possible for replicas to be produced.

LOTUS TYPE 29 SPECIFICATIONS

ENGINE:
All aluminium V-8 256 inch (3.76 x 2.87) pushrod valve train. Four dual-downdraft Webers, distributor ignition, three Bendix fuel pumps and dry-sump lube system. 376 bhp @ 7200 rpm

TRANSMISSION:
Four-speed Colotti Type 37A with individual lube system. Triple disc Borg & Beck clutch of 7.5 inches diameter. Open two-joint driveshafts with recirculating-ball splines.

CHASSIS:
Stress-skin, rivetted and constructed from 16-gauge aluminium, with steel cross-members.

STEERING:
Lotus rack-and-pinion, 2 and a quarter turns from lock to lock

FRONT SUSPENSION:
Lower A-Arm, single upper levering on inboard-mounted coil/shocks, rack and pinion steering and anti-sway bar

REAR SUSPENSION:
Reversed lower wishbones, top links, twin radius rods, outboard-mounted coil/shocks and anti-sway bar

TYRES:
Dunlops fitted for testing, Firestone in the Indy race

DIMENSIONS:

Wheelbase	96 inches
Front & Rear track	56 inches
Overall length	150 inches
Overall height	30.5 inches
Ground clearance	3.75 inches
Wet weight	1130 pounds
Oil storage	4.8 gallons
Gas tanks	50 gallons
Weight distribution	60% rear
	40% front

Viewed from above a pair of Lotus 29s. No. 92 is seen with the nose of No. 91 just visible

TYPE 29

LOTUS 29 RACING RECORD

DATE	EVENT	DRIVER	CAR NO.	CHASSIS NO.	RESULT
30th May 1963	Indianapolis 500	Jim Clark	92	29/3	2nd
30th May 1963	Indianapolis 500	Dan Gurney	93	29/1	7th
30th May 1963	Indianapolis 500	Dan Gurney	91	29/2	–
18th August 1963	Milwaukee 200	Jim Clark	92	29/3	1st
18th August 1963	Milwaukee 200	Dan Gurney	93	29/1	3rd
22nd September 1963	Trenton 200	Jim Clark	92	29/3	21st
22nd September 1963	Trenton 200	Dan Gurney	93	29/1	16th
30th May 1964	Indianapolis 500	Bobby Marshman	51	29/2	25th
23rd August 1964	Milwaukee 200	Bobby Marshman	51	29/2	24th
31st May 1965	Indianapolis 500	Al Miller	74	29/2	4th

Al Miller drove for Jerry Aldermann and finished fourth in the 1965 Indy 500 where he averaged 146.6 mph for the 200 laps. Marshman's fatal accident was in a Lotus 29.

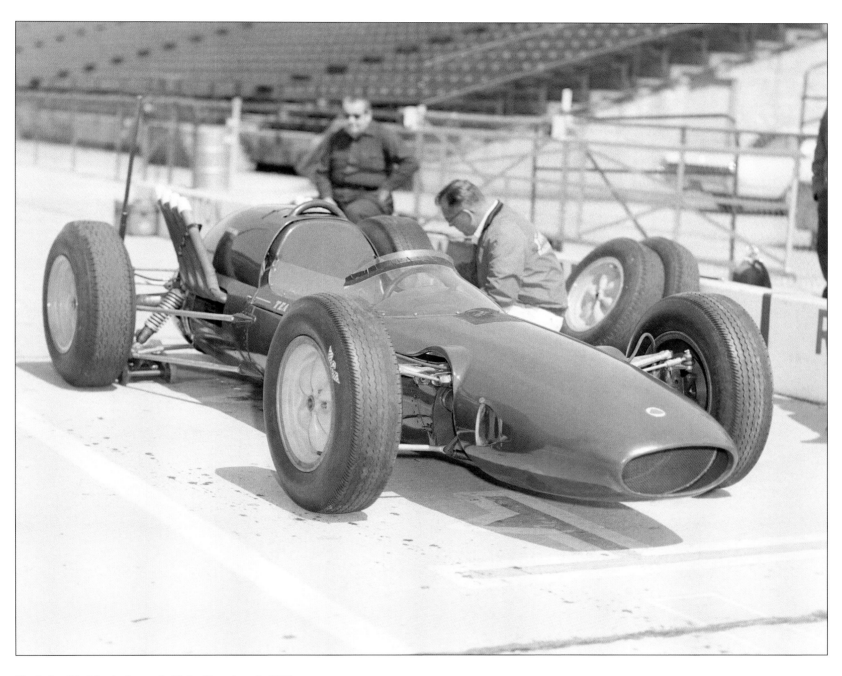

The Lotus 29 at the Indianapolis Motor Speedway in 1963

Jim Clark's Lotus 29/3 had race number 92 at the 1963 Indianapolis Motor speedway he qualified 5th and came 2nd place in the race itself, behind Parnelli Jones. Jim Clark's second place finish with an average speed of 142.752 mph was only 34 seconds behind winner Parnelli Jones who averaged 143.137 mph for the distance. Dan Gurney finished 7th in Lotus 29/1

FIRST INDIANAPOLIS CAR

Jim Clark's second place in the 1963 Indianapolis event was spectacular because it not only bettered all previous times for Indy 500 winners but also achieved the best time ever recorded by a rear-engined car. On lap 68 the Lotus-Fords had climbed to number one and two positions, and Jim Clark established race records on the 70th, 80th and 90th laps.

For the Indy 500, Jim Clark's car was British Racing Green in colour with a yellow stripe topside and around the nose cowling. Clark's car was chassis 29/3 and ran as number 92 as can be seen in the photograph.

At Milwaukee on 18 August 1963, two Lotus-Fords were entered in the 200 mile Tony Bettenhauser Memorial Race and finished first and third. Jim Clark in Lotus 29/3 established a new 200 mile record of 104.48 mph.

At the end of 1963 the Lotus 29 that Dan Gurney had crashed in qualifying for the 1963 Indy was sold through Ford to Lindsey Hopkins.

Parnelli Jones won the 1963 Indy with Jim Clark second and A.J. Foyt third.

LOTUS TYPE 30 SPECIFICATIONS

ENGINE:
Ford 289 Fairlane V8 cast-iron block

GEARBOX:
ZF 5-speed All synchromesh

FRONT SUSPENSION:
Unequal length double wishbones, coil springs and Armstrong adjustable dampers

REAR SUSPENSION:
wishbones with single lower radius arm, coil spring and Armstrong adjustable dampers

STEERING:
Rack and pinion, adjustable column

CLUTCH:
Laycock twin dry plates of 8.5 inch diameter

PRODUCED:
33 cars

TORQUE:
278 lb-ft @4500 rpm

POWER:
350 bhp @ 6500 rpm

DIMENSIONS:

Wheelbase	7ft 10.5 inches
Front and rear track	4ft 5 inches
Overall length	13ft 9 inches
Overall width	5ft 8 inches
Ground clearance	4.5 inches

Design of the Lotus 30 was handed over to the draughtsman, as Len Terry had told Colin Chapman the chassis would not be stiff enough among other weaknesses. Colin Chapman would not accept some of Len Terry's other criticisms. The Lotus 30's poor racing record probably proved Len Terry right.

The Power unit of the Lotus Type 30 is mounted in the rear position, and is based on the Ford Fairline 4727 cc V8 engine and is fairly similar to that fitted in the AC Cobra.

The regulations for prototype racing in respect of seating dimensions and door apertures were quite stringent. Colin Chapman therefore decided to use a backbone type of frame as used on the Lotus Elan. The chassis is shaped like a tuning fork. The central backbone, fabricated from 16-gauge steel sheet, later on 18-gauge panelling, forms an enormously rigid box of trapezoidal section, 6 inches wide at the top, 8.5 inches at the bottom and 10.5 inches deep. Its sides continue downwards forming the sides of an inverted channel which carries two water pipes, two oil pipes, the brake and clutch hydraulic lines, the throttle cable and the wiring harness.

From 1965 a Mark 2 Lotus 30 became available, on which access to the transmission was easier. Jim Clark gained second place at Aintree with the Lotus 30, and twelfth place at the Tourist Trophy on 29th August 1964 in car number one having completed one hundred and thirteen laps.

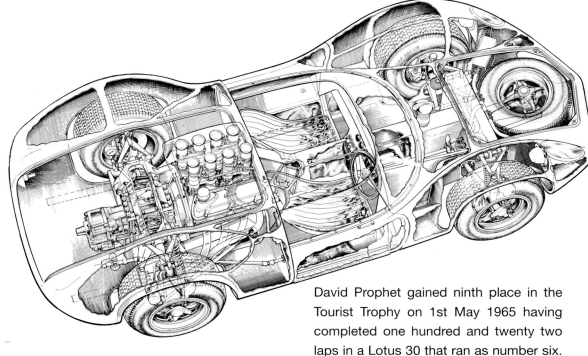

David Prophet gained ninth place in the Tourist Trophy on 1st May 1965 having completed one hundred and twenty two laps in a Lotus 30 that ran as number six.

Colin Chapman decided to build a fairly simple and more easily repairable car for Formula 3. He decided to reserve the more expensive monocoque car for Formula 2.

The chassis is of round and square section tubing with a bulkhead fitted at the forward end of the cockpit. This holds the instruments and the steering column bracket.

The front suspension is by unequal length double wishbones, an anti-roll bar and outboard mounted Armstrong coil spring/damper units. The rear suspension is by the Lotus system of single upper links, reversed lower wishbones, double parallel radius arms, anti-roll bar and coil spring/damper units.

On the Lotus 31 Girling disc brakes are fitted all round and are outboard mounted.

Cosworth MAE engines only became available from 1965, earlier Lotus 31s having the Holbay modified Ford unit.

Few top drivers chose the Lotus 31 for Formula 3 and most of the cars went to racing driving schools. The Jim Russell School at Snetterton purchased ten Lotus 31s for training pupils while Motor Racing Stables at Brands Hatch operated four Lotus 31s for their regular Friday training sessions.

LOTUS TYPE 31 SPECIFICATIONS

ENGINE:

Type	Cosworth 998 cc
Bore	81 mm
Stroke	48.4 mm

MAXIMUM POWER:
95 bhp at 8700 rpm

CHASSIS:
Multi-tubular space-frame

GEARBOX:
Original VW or Renault four-speed gearbox but later MK VI Hewland gearbox

DIMENSIONS:

Wheelbase	7ft 6 inches
Front track	4ft 3.5 inches
Rear track	4ft 2 inches
Overall length	11ft 7 inches
Overall width	2ft 4 inches
Kerb weight	882 lb

TYPE 32 AND 32B

The Lotus Type 32 was similar in dimensions to the Lotus 25 and the late Lotus 33 models. This car had a monocoque chassis unit with "D" shaped longerons at each side of the chassis, located at the front and rear by load bearing box members. Flexible rubber fuel tanks were incorporated in the "D" shaped chassis side members giving a total fuel capacity of 18 gallons.

The Lotus 32B was a special version of the Lotus 32 built for the Tasman Formula. The Tasman Formula was a series of races held during the summer in Australia and New Zealand. The Lotus 32B had a 2495 cc Coventry Climax engine. Jim Clark gained five victories in the Tasman series.

A works backed team of cars raced by the Ron Harris team in 1964 gained a number of successes. Jim Clark won the Pau Grand Prix in the Lotus 32 in a time of 2h 12m 476s while in the same race Peter Arundell's Lotus 27 gained third place.

Jim Clark also won the Eifelrennen in Germany and the Guards Trophy F2 race at Brands Hatch. Team mate Mike Spence won the F2 section of the Aintree 200 race and Peter Proctor finished second in the Vienna Grand Prix and the Circuit of Berlin race. Jackie Stewart finished second in the Ile de France race at Montlhery.

The team was somewhat hampered because Clark and Spence were often engaged in other races.

On the Lotus 32 outboard Girling brakes were used, and the gearbox was either a Hewland Mark IV or a Hewland Mark VII. On the Lotus 32B a ZF 5 DS gearbox was used.

LOTUS TYPE 32 SPECIFICATIONS

ENGINE:
Cosworth-Ford SCA 998 cc
Bore and stroke   81 mm x 48.4 mm
Maximum power   115 bhp 8700 rpm
Compression ratio   12.5 to 1

FRONT SUSPENSION:
Upper lever arm, lower wishbones, inboard coil spring, damper units

REAR SUSPENSION:
Single upper links, reversed lower wishbones, double radius arms and coil spring/damper units

CHASSIS:
Aluminium monocoque

DIMENSIONS:
Wheelbase   7ft 9.5 inches
Front track   4ft 0.4165 inches
Rear track   4ft 7.1875 inches
Overall length   11ft 7 inches

FRONT BRAKES:
Girling disc 10.50 inches diameter

KERB WEIGHT:
926 lb

LOTUS TYPE 32 RACING RECORD

DATE	EVENT	RESULT
5th April 1964	Pau Grand Prix (F2)	1st
26th April 1964	Eifelrennen (F2)	1st
5th July 1964	Rheims G.P.	4th
3rd August 1964	British Eagle Trophy	1st
9th August 1964	Canon Race (F2)	2nd
13th September 1964	Albi G.P.	Retired
19th September 1964	Gold Cup (F2)	2nd
10th January 1965	New Zealand G.P.	Retired
16th January 1965	Tasman Cup	1st
23rd January 1965	Lady Wigram Trophy	1st
30th January 1965	Teretonga Trophy	1st
14th February 1965	Tasman Cup	1st
21st February 1965	Tasman Cup	2nd
1st March 1965	Tasman Cup	5th
7th March 1965	Tasman Cup	1st
10th April 1965	Formula 2 (Snetterton)	3rd
25th April 1965	Pau Grand Prix (F2)	1st
7th June 1965	London Trophy (F2)	1st

The first Lotus Type 33, chassis R8, was driven by Jim Clark in the 1964 Aintree 200 where it made its first appearance. Jim Clark was in second place when he crashed into a slower car. Jim Clark was unhurt but the car was badly damaged and did not reappear until later in the year.

The Lotus Type 33B, chassis R10, first appeared in the South African Grand Prix on 1st January 1965 but was subsequently written off at Brands Hatch on 13 March 1965. Team Lotus were left with two Type 33s, chassis numbers R7 and R9.

The Lotus 33 was still being used by Team Lotus in the early part of 1967. Graham Hill achieved second place at the Monaco Grand Prix of 1967 in a Lotus 33 while Jim Clark won the Tasman Championship in 1967 with the Lotus 33. Mike Spence came 8th at the German Grand Prix on 2 August 1964 with his Lotus 33.

LOTUS TYPE 33 GRAND PRIX WINS

1965	South African Grand Prix
1965	Belgian Grand Prix
1965	British Grand Prix
1965	Dutch Grand Prix
1965	German Grand Prix

Each time driven to victory by Jimmy Clark

LOTUS TYPE 33 SPECIFICATIONS

ENGINE:

Type	Coventry Climax FWMV
Bore	67.8 mm
Stroke	51.6 mm
Cubic capacity	1496 cc
Compression ratio	11.5 to 1
Maximum power	200 bhp @ 9600 rpm

TRANSMISSION:
ZF 5D510 five-speed gearbox

CHASSIS:
Monocoque in light alloy

DIMENSIONS:

Wheelbase	7ft 8 inches
Front track	4ft 7 inches
Rear track	4ft 8 inches
Overall length	11ft 10 inches

Lotus 33 driver Mike Spence had success at the 1965 Brands Hatch Race of Champions. This was unusual for a Lotus number two driver.

LOTUS 33 SUCCESSES

DRIVER	CAR	CHASSIS NO.	PLACE	EVENT	DATE
Jim Clark	Lotus 33	Chassis R8	1st	Solitude Grand Prix	19th July 1964
Mike Spence	Lotus 33	Chassis R9	1st	Race of Champions	13th March 1965
Jim Clark	Lotus 33	Chassis R9	1st	Dutch Grand Prix	18th July 1965
Jim Clark	Lotus 33	Chassis R10	1st	South African Grand Prix	1st January 1965
Jim Clark	Lotus 33	Chassis R11	1st	Syracuse Grand Prix	4th April 1965
Jim Clark	Lotus 33	Chassis R11	1st	Belgian Grand Prix	13th June 1965
Jim Clark	Lotus 33	Chassis R11	1st	British Grand Prix	10th July 1965
Jim Clark	Lotus 33	Chassis R11	1st	German Grand Prix	1st August 1965
Jim Clark	Lotus 33	Chassis R11	1st	South African Grand Prix	1st January 1966
Jim Clark	Lotus 33	Chassis R12	1st	Warwick Farm	14th February 1966
Leo Geoghegan	Lotus 33	Chassis R12	1st	Sandown Park	17th September 1967
Leo Geoghegan	Lotus 33	Chassis R12	1st	Mallahla	14th October 1968
Leo Geoghegan	Lotus 33	Chassis R12	1st	Japanese Grand Prix	3rd May 1969
Jim Clark	Lotus 33	Chassis R14	1st	Levin	14th January 1967
Jim Clark	Lotus 33	Chassis R14	1st	Lady Wigram Trophy	21st January 1967
Jim Clark	Lotus 33	Chassis R14	1st	Teretonga	28th January 1967
Jim Clark	Lotus 33	Chassis R14	1st	Lakeside	12th February 1967
Jim Clark	Lotus 33	Chassis R14	1st	Sandown Park	26th February 1967

Chassis sequence of the Lotus 33 carried on from the visually similar Lotus 25.

The Lotus Type 34 appeared in 1964, and was in effect a slightly modified version of the Lotus 29.

There were great hopes after Jim Clark's Lotus Ford had qualified for pole position. But the 48th Indianapolis 500 was red-flagged and halted when the race was marred by one of the worst pile-ups in the history of the brickyard. Seven cars were eliminated and two drivers – Dave McDonald and Eddie Sachs were killed.

On the restart, Jim Clark went ahead once more. Tread from the Dunlop D12 tyre became problematic and the unbalancing caused a drive shaft to break loose. It took Jim Clark a quarter of a lap to halt the car which he did safely.

A.J. Foyt's car, the Sheraton-Thompson Watson Offenhauser won the race. In 1965 A.J. Foyt drove a Lotus 34 into second place at the Indianapolis 500.

LOTUS TYPE 34 SPECIFICATIONS

ENGINE:
Ford Quad-Cam V8 aluminium crankcase and block

CUBIC CAPACITY:
4195 cc

BORE AND STROKE:
3.76 x 2.87 inches

COMPRESSION RATIO:
14 to 1

TRANSMISSION:
ZF 2 DS 20 2-speed gearbox

FRONT SUSPENSION:
Chassis offset 2.375 inches to the left by means of longer suspension links on right-hand side. Cantilever top rocking arms operating inboard coil spring/Monroe co-axial damper unit with lower wishbone

REAR SUSPENSION:
Reversed lower wishbone with single chassis mounting. Single top arm. Unequal length twin radius arms. Offset chassis achieved by extending chassis pick-up points on right-hand side

STEERING:
Lotus rack-and-pinion, Springall steering wheel. Lock to lock required two and a quarter turns

DIMENSIONS:

Wheelbase	96 inches
Front track	56 inches
Rear track	56 inches
Overall length	12ft 6 inches
Weight	1200 lbs

Dan Gurney's white and blue US-liveried Lotus Ford Type 34 ready to be fuelled at the Humble depot in Gasoline Alley.

Jim Clark in his Lotus 34 after his new qualifying record of 158.828 mph. Tyre trouble forced him to retire from the race itself.

Lotus 35 at the 1966 Pau Grand Prix

The Lotus 35 of 1965 had evolved from the Lotus 27 and Lotus 32 monocoques. The Coventry Climax 2.5 FPF engine could be fitted to the car for Tasman racing. At the start of the season Ron Harris, who looked after the participation of Team Lotus, used both Lotus 35s and Lotus 32s. Drivers included Jim Clark, Brian Hart, Mike Spence and Peter Revson, the latter winning the F3 race at Monaco with a Lotus 35.

The Lotus Type 36 was the second type number to be allocated to a Lotus Elan, and was given to the Series 3 fixed-head coupe that came out in September 1965. This Lotus Elan had a four-speed gearbox and a final drive ratio of 3.55 to 1. The boot lid extended to the rear edge of the rear deck.

The Lotus Type "Three-Seven" was shown at the 1965 racing Car Show and was in effect a much-modified Lotus Seven Series II. Only one model of the Lotus "Three-Seven" was built but it was raced with some success by John Berry, a Lotus Cars sales manager. He won the Lotus Seven Trophy for 1965, and he attained 8 firsts, 6 seconds, 4 thirds, 4 fourths and 2 fifths with the car.

TYPE 38

The Lotus Type 38 was designed by Len Terry and it was a true monocoque and the 38's metalwork wrapped right over the drivers knees. There were three fuel tanks and Len Terry designed them so that they drained from the right side first. This was to keep as much of the weight as possible on the inboard side for as long as possible.

Indianapolis regulations required two compulsory pit stops. At Indianapolis in 1965, the Team Lotus cars were driven by Jim Clark and Bobby Johns.

On 31st May 1965 Jim Clark won at Indianapolis and secured his biggest pay cheque ever. His average speed was 150.686 mph. Bobby Johns came 8th at Indianapolis in 1965.

David Lazenby was the Project Engineer for the Indianapolis car and was the Lotus Chief Mechanic for the event. The actual car was built and maintained by David Lazenby, Graham Clode, Mike Underwood, and Jim Smith, and this was chassis number 38/1. A total of ten cars were built.

LOTUS TYPE 38 SPECIFICATIONS

ENGINE:
Ford Quad-cam V8 aluminium crankcase, block & heads

CUBIC CAPACITY:
4195 cc

BORE AND STROKE:
3.76 x 2.87 inches

COMPRESSION RATIO:
12.5 to 1

TRANSMISSION:
ZF 2 DS 20 2-speed gearbox

FIRST- HAND VIEW

Len Terry on the Lotus 38

"When the gravity feed regulations became known, it was obviously a matter of vital importance to increase the replenishment flow during pit stops to gain an advantage, and it became clear later that no one else within the other teams had considered a solution too deeply. I based my design on a venturi shape for the 3-inch-diameter outlet that fed into a "y" from which two 3-inch lines individually fed fuel to each side of the car. My calculations promised a delivery of 50 US gallons in under 20 seconds, and if no one else thought of a similar scheme we would gain an enormous advantage. Fortunately, no one else did ... "

TYPE 38

TYPE 38 RACING RECORD

DATE	EVENT	DRIVER.	CAR NO.	CHASSIS NO.	RACE RESULT
31st May 1965	Indianapolis 500	Jim Clark	82	38/1	1st
31st May 1965	Indianapolis 500	Bobby Johns	83	38/2	7th
31st May 1965	Indianapolis 500	Dan Gurney	17	38/3	26th
30th May 1966	Indianapolis 500	Jim Clark	19	38/4	2nd
30th May 1966	Indianapolis 500	Al Unser	18	38/7	12th
30th May 1966	Indianapolis 500	A.J. Foyt	2	38/6	26th
30th May 1966	Indianapolis 500	Mario Andretti	1	38/5	Not Raced
30th May 1967	Indianapolis 500	Larry Dickson	22	38/3	15th
30th May 1967	Indianapolis 500	Jim Clark	31	38/7	31st
30th May 1967	Indianapolis 500	Graham Hill	80	38/8/5	Car set aside

LOTUS TYPE 38 SUSPENSION

FRONT SUSPENSION:

Chassis offset 3 inches to left by means of longer suspension links on right hand side. Welded up cantilver top rocking arms operating inboard coil spring / monroe co-axial damper unit with lower wishbone.

REAR SUSPENSION:

Single top arm and reversed lower wishbone with single chassis mounting. Unequal length twin radius arms. Outboard coil spring / 72 monroe co-axial damper unit. Unlike the Type 29 and Type 34 chassis off-set was effected by longer top link and lower wishbone on right hand side.

Jim Clark in chassis 38/7. He is seen here in the 1967 Indy 500 archive photograph. Len Terry was given carte blanche to design the Lotus 38 as Colin Chapman was involved with the Tasman Series.

The Lotus Type 39 was the car used by Jim Clark in the 1966 Tasman Series where he won at Warwick Farm, came second at Levin and Sandown Park and came third in the Lady Wigram Trophy.

The two and a half litre BRM of Jackie Stewart dominated the series and the Lotus 39 was no real match.

Leo Geoghegan acquired the Lotus 39 from Colin Chapman in 1967 and he ran the car in the Tasman Championship for several years up until 1970.

LOTUS TYPE 39 SPECIFICATIONS

ENGINE:
Coventry Climax FPF

CUBIC CAPACITY:
2495 cc

GEARBOX:
Hewland 5-speed

CHASSIS:
Aluminium alloy monocoque

DIMENSIONS:
Wheelbase	7ft 7.5 inches
Length	11ft 8 inches

PRODUCTION:
1 car

LOTUS TYPE 39 RACING RECORD

8th January 1966	New Zealand G.P.	Retired
15th January 1966	Gold Leaf Trophy	2nd
22nd January 1966	Lady Wigram Trophy	Retired
29th January 1966	Teretonga Trophy	Retired
13th February 1966	Tasman Cup Race	1st
20th February 1966	Australian G.P.	3rd
27 February 1966	Tasman Cup Race	2nd
6th March 1966	Tasman Cup Race	7th

The Lotus Type 40 made its debut at the Austrian Grand Prix on 22 August 1965 from which it retired.

Although the body shape is not vastly different from the Lotus 30, there is a longer nose to prevent lifting at high speed.

Compared to the Lotus 30 the Lotus 40 was a considerably more beefed up sports car. The wishbones were increased in size and strength and new 11.25 inch diameter ventilated disc brakes were fitted.

The Lotus 40 could not match the Lola T70s nor the McLaren Elva Oldsmobiles, and in April 1966 Lotus Components put its two works Lotus 40s up for sale at £3750 each. The Lotus 40 was the last Sports Racer Lotus made.

Jack Sears states the Lotus 40 was put on the drawing board quickly and that he was hauled in to try the car with its 5.3 litre engine. He recalls that it was Richie Ginther who famously described the Lotus 40 as "a 30 with 10 more mistakes".

LOTUS TYPE 40 SPECIFICATIONS

ENGINE:
Ford V8

CUBIC CAPACITY
5295 cc and 5754 cc

GEARBOX:
Hewland LG500

CHASSIS:
Girder box-section

DIMENSIONS:
Wheelbase	7ft 10.5 inches
Length	13ft 9 inches

PRODUCTION:
3 cars

Above: Jim Clark in the Lotus 40

LOTUS TYPE 41 SPECIFICATIONS

ENGINE:
Cosworth-Ford MAE

GEARBOX:
Hewland four-speed and reverse

CHASSIS:
Space-frame tubular

FRONT/REAR WHEELS:
13 inch magnesium

FRONT/REAR BRAKES:
10.5 inch Girling disc

DIMENSIONS:

Length	144 inches
Width	66 inches
Wheelbase	90 inches
Front track	56.5 inches
Rear track	56 inches
Ground clearance	3.5 inches
Height	27.75 inches over crash bar

ORIGINAL COST:

£2475

Jackie Oliver came sixth in the Crystal Palace F2 race of 1967.

The Lotus 41 was their Formula 3 car for 1966 and for this they went back to the space-frame tubular chassis. There was extensive use of sheet metal in the foot box, cockpit, gearbox mounting and undertray.

Suspension was conventional with use of double wishbones and coil spring suspension units at the front, and radius arms, lower wishbone and top arm at the rear. Spherical bearings were used on the rear suspension and nylon bearings on the front suspension.

A team of these cars were run by Charles Lucas Engineering Ltd under the team name "Charles Lucas Team Lotus". Piers Courage headed the team of drivers that also included American Roy Pike and Mo Nunn.

A Lotus 41B was used in American Formula B racing and in 1967 the car was a Lotus 41C. In 1968 the car used by John Miles was the Lotus 41X which scored four wins, including victory in the 1968 Silverstone International Trophy meeting.

LOTUS TYPE 42 SPECIFICATIONS

ENGINE:
BRM H16 with light alloy crankcase and cylinder heads

CUBIC CAPACITY:
4198 cc

BORE AND STROKE:
2.94 x 2.36 inches

TRANSMISSION:
BRM 3-speed

FRONT SUSPENSION:
Chassis offset 3 inches to left by means of longer suspension links on right-hand side Welded-up cantilever top rocking arms operating inboard coil-spring/Monroe co-axial damper units with lower wishbones

REAR SUSPENSION:
Reversed lower wishbone with single chassis mounting, single top arm, and unequal length twin radius arms. Outboard coil-spring/Monroe co-axial damper units

DIMENSIONS:

Wheelbase	96 inches
Front track	60 inches
Rear track	60 inches
Overall length	13ft 6 inches (or 14ft 4 inches)
Weight	1350 lbs

The Lotus Type 42 was the first car designed for Team Lotus by Maurice Phillippe who replaced Len Terry as Lotus Chief Designer.

The Lotus 42 was originally designed to take the BRM H16 engine but the H16 engines were plagued by problems and did not materialise. When it was confirmed there would be no BRM engine one car was converted to take an Indy Ford V8 engine. The Ford V8 engine was longer than the BRM engine and the Type 42's overall length with the Ford V8 engine was 14ft 4 inches compared to 13ft 6 inches with the BRM unit.

Two Lotus 42s were built and given chassis numbers 42B/1 and 42B/2. Chassis number 42B/1 was given the race number 81 as seen in the photograph below, while chassis number 42B/2 was given the race number 30. Chassis number 42B/1, later 42F/1, was the car that was classified 32nd at the 1967 Indianapolis 500 mile race, driven by Graham Hill.

Graham Hill in the Lotus Type 42F. In the Indianapolis 500 Mile Race of 1967 this car only achieved 31st on the grid.
In the race itself, piston trouble forced Graham Hill to drop out after just twenty three laps.

Jim Clark's unexpected victory in the 1966 United States Grand Prix gave him a first prize that was worth more than what Jack Brabham had picked up for all his four Grand Prix victories.

LOTUS TYPE 43 RACING RECORD

DATE	EVENT	DRIVER	RESULTS
4th September 1966	Italian Grand Prix	Jim Clark	Retired
2nd October 1966	United States Grand Prix	Jim Clark	1st
23rd October 1966	Mexican Grand Prix	Jim Clark	Retired
2nd January 1967	South African Grand Prix	Jim Clark	Retired
2nd January 1967	South African Grand Prix	Graham Hill	Retired

LOTUS TYPE 43 SPECIFICATIONS

ENGINE:
BRM H-16

GEAR BOX:
BRM 6-speed

CHASSIS:
Stressed monocoque

FRONT WHEELS: 15 x 8.5 inches
REAR WHEELS: 15 x 9.5 inches
FRONT BRAKES: 12 inch ventilated discs
REAR BRAKES: 12 inch ventilated discs

DIMENSIONS:
Wheelbase   8ft
Track   5ft
Height   2ft 6.5 inches

PRODUCTION:
2 cars

FRONT SUSPENSION:
Top rocker arm, lower wishbone.

REAR SUSPENSION:
Reverse lower wishbone, top link twin radius arms.

The Lotus Type 43 was built to take BRM's H16 engine and was also fitted with a six-speed BRM gearbox.

Jim Clark had dominated the 1965 Grand Prix, and had won the World Championship for the second time, but since then he had not had much success. This was to change on the 2nd October 1966 and after a year gap Jim Clark won another grand prix. Jim Clark's victory was also the first time that the chequered flag had fallen for a car fitted with the 3-litre BRM engine.

The chances of this happening must have been remote. Although Graham Hill had demonstrated the potential of this engine at Monza in the Italian Grand Prix by getting to fifth place at one time, in practice for the United States Grand Prix itself Clark broke his engine.

And it was only because the works BRM's finished final training in good order that Tony Rudd was able to offer their spare unit to Colin Chapman.

Given the overnight task of engine installation by Lotus mechanics, it was still not known even minutes before the race whether Clark would drive the 3-litre car or one of the team's 2-litre machines.

Jim Clark's win at the U.S. Grand Prix was achieved in a time of 2 hours 9 minutes 40.1 seconds.

Jim Clark retired with engine problems on the Lotus's 44's debut at Barcelona, and the other eight drivers who tried the Lotus 44 faired little better.

LOTUS TYPE 44 SPECIFICATIONS

ENGINE:
Ford Cosworth SCA

GEARBOX:
Hewland Mark IV or Mark VI

CHASSIS:
Aluminium monocoque

FRONT WHEELS: 13 x 7 inches

PRODUCTION:
3 cars

DIMENSIONS:
Wheelbase   7ft 9.5 inches
Overall length   12ft 3 inches
Maximum track   4ft 6 inches

REAR WHEELS: 13 x 10 inches

Jim Clark continued to have a bad season with the Formula 2 type 44 during 1966, largely due to the fact the car was no match for Brabham - Honda's.

Lotus Elans were designated either the Type 26, Type 36, Type 45 or Type 50 and the chassis identification chart below shows why this was the case.

The Lotus Type 45 was the designation given to the drop head version of the Series 3, which arrived in mid-1966. Revisions included a wrap-over boot lid, new doors and framed side windows which were now electrically operated. A folding hood also replaced the lift-off item.

LOTUS ELAN CHASSIS NUMBERS

DATE	CHASSIS NO.	
January 1963	26/0001	Elan 1500 introduced
May 1963	26/0026	Hardtop optional
January 1964	26/0330	Model continues
November 1964	26/3901	Series 2 introduced
January 1965	26/4325	Series 2 continues
September 1965	36/4510	Series 3 fhc introduced
November 1965	36/5147	Close ratio gearbox available
January 1966	26/5207	Convertible continues
	36/5201	Fhc continues
	26/5282	Special equipment convertible available
June 1966	26/5810	S2 convertible final chassis number
	26/5798	S2 conv. (special equipment) final chassis number
	45/4702	S3 convertible introduced
	45/5701	S3 conv (special equipment) introduced
July 1966	36/5977	S3 fhc (special equipment) introduced
January 1967	45/6678	S3 convertible continued
	45/6680	S3 conv (special equipment) continued
	36/6679	S3 fhc continued
	36/6683	S3 fhc (special equipment) continued
June 1967	51/0001	+2 fhc introduced
August 1967	45/7328	Convertible continued
	45/7329	Convertible (special equipment) continued
	36/7327	Fhc continued
	36/7331	Fhc (special equipment) continued
March 1968	45/7895	S4 convertible introduced
	36/7895	S4 fhc introduced
November 1968	50/1280	Stromberg carbs introduced on +2 fhc
	45/8600	Stromberg carbs introduced on convertible
	45/8600	Stromberg carbs introduced on fhc
March 1969	50/1554	+2 fhc introduced
August 1969	45/9524	Weber carbs re-introduced on convertible
	36/9524	Weber carbs re-introduced on fhc
December 1969	50/2407	+2 final chassis number
	50/2536	Final number of old numbering (+2S)
	45/9824	Final number of old numbering (conv.)
	36/9824	Final number of old numbering (fhc)
January 1970	7001 010001	All models continued with a suffix to identify each one i.e. S4 fhc = A; S4 fhc (special equipment) = E; S4 convertible = C; S4 convertible (special equipment) = G; +2S fhc = L; 7001 = 1970 January
February 1971	7101	Spring version introduced on fhc and convertible; +2S 130 introduced
January 1972	7201	Models continue unchanged
October 1972	–	5-speed gearbox optional on +2S 130
January 1973	7301	Convertible and fhc continued
	7301 1132	+2S 130 and +2S 130/5 continued
August 1973	7301	Elan convertible and fhc discontinued

LOTUS TYPE 45 SPECIFICATIONS

ENGINE:
Lotus-Ford twin-cam

CUBIC CAPACITY:
1558 cc

GEARBOX:
Ford 4-speed

CHASSIS:
Folded steel backbone

DIMENSIONS:
Wheelbase	7ft
Track	4ft

The Lotus Elan Sprint had a compression ratio of 10.3 to 1 as against the Lotus Elan S1 to S4's compression ratio of 9.5 to 1. The power of the Lotus Elan Sprint was 126 bhp at 6500 rpm.

LOTUS TYPE 46

SPECIFICATIONS

ENGINE:

Type	Renault 16 water-water-cooled 4-cylinder
Bore	76 mm (2.99) inches
Stroke	81 mm (3.19) inches
Cubic capacity	1470 cc
Compression ratio	10.25 to 1

GEARBOX:
Renault 4-speed

FRONT SUSPENSION:
Independent, coil spring/damper units, upper and lower wishbones, anti-roll bar

REAR SUSPENSION:
Independent coil spring/damper units, longitudinal radius arms, lower transverse links, fixed length drive shafts

DIMENSIONS:

Wheelbase	7ft 7.5 inches
Length	13ft 0.0714 inches
Width	5ft 4.375 inches
Height	3ft 7 inches

LOTUS TYPE 47

This car had a Lotus-Cosworth 1594 cc engine and a Hewland FT200 gearbox

LOTUS TYPE 47D

This car had a Rover V8 3.5 litre engine and a ZF five-speed gearbox. Under the auspices of racing mechanic Norman Birkenshaw the car was developed into a 4.4 litre V8.

The Lotus Europa Type 46 went into production in March 1967, and the improved Series 2 version, know as the Type 54, made its first appearance in May 1968.

The Lotus Europa, code-named the P.5, was a mid-engined sports car, and it is hard to believe that any production car could be three feet seven and a half inches tall. The rear bumper was as high as the bonnet and the window sills. The body was moulded in glass-fibre, and was mounted on the chassis through a number of rubber-insulated attachments. The Europa's unusual styling was the work of John Frayling, who was responsible for the Lotus Elan Coupe.

The Type 47 Europa was directly developed from the Type 46 and was a pure competition car for Group 4. It achieved considerable success in the hands of John Miles and won the 2 litre Prototype class at the 1967 BOAC 500 race. At the Watkins Glen 6-Hours on 11th July 1970 Jim Bandy/Bruce Cargill gained 14th place. At the Brands Hatch 6 Hours, on 7th April 1968 Jackie Oliver and John Miles gained tenth place after completing two hundred and two laps in car number twenty four.

LOTUS EUROPA TYPE 47 RACING RECORD

DATE	EVENT	CAR NO.	DRIVERS	LAPS COMPLETED	RACE RESULT
30th July 1967	Brands Hatch 6 Hrs	29	John Jeremy Miles Jackie Oliver	197	9th
30th July 1967	Brands Hatch 6 Hrs	30	Trevor Taylor David Preston	178	19th
30th July 1967	Brands Hatch 6 Hrs	32	John Hine Keith Greene	56	Did not finish (Engine)
3rd September 1967	Nürburgring 500 kms	9	Trevor Taylor	17	Not running at finish
3rd September 1967	Nürburgring 500 kms	12	John Hine		Did not finish
23rd March 1968	Sebring 12 Hrs	68	Earl Sylvia Dave Domizi Robert Fogle	81	Did not finish (Accident)
7th April 1968	Brands Hatch 6 Hrs	24	Jackie Oliver John Jeremy Miles	202	10th
7th April 1968	Brands Hatch 6 Hrs	41	Andrew Hedges Julian Sutton	200	13th
7th April 1968	Brands Hatch 6 Hrs	27	Peter Jackson Geoffrey Oliver	42	Did not finish (Overheating)
7th April 1968	Brands Hatch 6 Hrs	25	Trevor Taylor Mike Budge	35	Did not finish (Gearbox)
7th April 1968	Brands Hatch 6 Hrs	26	John Hine Mike Crabtree		Did not finish (Fuel leak)
19th May 1968	Nürburgring 1000 kms	91	Peter Jackson Rhoddy Harvey-Bailey	37	32nd
19th May 1968	Nürburgring 1000 kms	85	Trevor Taylor John Wagstaff		Did not finish (Fuel leak)
19th May 1968	Nürburgring 1000 kms	92	John Hine Mike Crabtree		Did not finish (Engine)
19th May 1968	Nürburgring 1000 kms	95	Peter Clarke Brian Alexander		Did not finish
19th May 1968	Nürburgring 1000 kms	103	Ragnar Eklund Per Brandstrom		Did not finish (Engine)

LOTUS EUROPA TYPE 47 RACING RECORD

DATE	EVENT	CAR NO.	DRIVERS	LAPS COMPLETED	RACE RESULT
26th May 1968	Spa Francorchamps 1000 Kms	53	Peter Jackson Clive Baker Roddy Harvey-Bailey	57	17th
26th May 1968	Spa Francorchamps 1000 Kms	52	John Hine Mike Crabtree	13	Did not finish (Exhaust)
14th July 1968	Watkins Glen 6 Hrs	47	Andre Prefontaine Peter Roberts	181	Did not finish
25th August 1968	Austrian Sports Car Grand Prix	18	Horst Mundschitz	63	Did not finish (Suspension)
22nd March 1969	Sebring 12 Hrs	69	Reggie Smith Tony Lilly Don Pickett	130	Not classified
1st June 1969	Nürburgring 1000 kms	70	Victor Walker Brian Alexander	35	26th
31st January 1970 to 1st February 1970	Daytona 24 Hrs	47	Jim Bandy Fred Stevenson Carl Williams	442	Did not finish (Engine)
21st March 1970	Sebring 12 Hrs	67	Jim Bandy Fred Stevenson	48	Did not finish (Wheel)
3rd May 1970	Targa Florio	194	Stefano Sebastiani Robero Nardini	7	47th
11th July 1970	Watkins Glen 6 Hrs	41	Jim Bandy Bruce Cargill	233	14th
11th October 1970	Österreichring 1000 Kms	16	Horst Mundschitz Gerhard Kramer		Did not finish
13th May 1973	Targa Florio	147	Brian Goellnicht Allan Girdler	6	Did not finish
1st-2nd February 1975	Daytona 24 Hrs	28	Anatoly Arutunoff Brian Goellnicht	114	Did not finish
31st January 1976 to 1st February 1976	Daytona 24 Hrs	28	Brian Goellnicht Anatoly Arutunoff	20	Did not finish
20th March 1976	Sebring 12 Hrs	8	Anatoly Arutunoff Jose Marina Jack May	162	26th

LOTUS EUROPA TYPE 47 RACING RECORD

DATE	EVENT	CAR NO.	DRIVERS	LAPS COMPLETED	RACE RESULT
20th March 1976	Sebring 12 Hrs	22	Tony Lilly Frank Marrs	97	Did not finish
5th-6th February 1977	Daytona 24 Hrs	98	Ralph Tolman Michael Brockman	50	Did not finish

In 1967 there was a Formula 2 for cars up to 1600 cc and it was for this that the Lotus Type 48 was developed.

The Lotus Type 48 first appeared in the Tasman series at the Australian Grand Prix. This event was held at Warwick Farm in February. Graham Hill gained fourth place in heat 1 of the April 1967 Spring Cup at Oulton Park, while at the September 1967 Gold Cup at Oulton Park he gained second place.

Jack Oliver won the Formula 2 Class in the German Grand Prix and gained fifth place overall on the 6th August 1967. This was in chasis 48/3. He drove a Lotus 48 sponsored by Herts and Essex Aero Club with some success. At the November 1967 Madrid G.P. in Jarama Alex Soler-Roig's Lotus 48 did not start

Jim Clark was tragically killed at Hockenheim while driving a Lotus 48 in April 1968.

LOTUS TYPE 48 SPECIFICATIONS

ENGINE:
Cosworth-Ford FVA
GEARBOX:
ZF5 DS12 5-speed
CUBIC CAPACITY:
1599 cc
DIMENSIONS:
Wheelbase   7ft 7.75 inches
Overall length   12ft 5.5 inches
CARS PRODUCED:
4
BRAKES: Outboard Girling Discs

A rear view of Graham Hill's Lotus 48 in which he set up the Formula Two lap record at Oulton Park on 15th April 1967.

LOTUS 48 AT THE GERMAN GRAND PRIX 1967

DRIVER	NUMBER	DATE	PRACTICE 1	PRACTICE 2	PRACTICE 3	RESULT	TIME
J. Oliver	24	6 August 1967	8m 54.10s	8m 40.90s	8m 34.90s	1st	2h 12m 04.90s

LOTUS TYPE 49 SPECIFICATIONS

ENGINE: V8 Cosworth, quad-cam.

Construction   Aluminium-alloy block and heads with steel wet liners, five main bearings with main bearing caps integral with sump, Cosworth-designed pistons manufactured by Hepolite, Vandervell lead indium main and big-end bearings

Bore x stroke   3.37 inches x 2.55 inches (85.7 mm x 64.8 mm)

Displacement   2993 cc

Compression ratio   11.0 to 1

Valve gear   Four valves per cylinder operated by gear-driven overhead camshafts per bank of cylinders

Fuel system   Lucas high-pressure port mechanical fuel injection

Ignition   Lucas, with Autolite spark plugs

Maximum power   409 bhp at 9000 rpm

TRANSMISSION: ZF 5-speed manual gearbox driving through ZF spiral bevel final drive with limited-slip differential, BRD tubular half shafts, Borg & Beck 7.25 inch diameter twin-plate clutch lined with Ferodo ceramic material; gearbox was later changed to a Hewland gearbox for increased reliability

Ratios   Varied according to circuit

BODY/CHASSIS: Aluminium monocoque skinned in 18-gauge L72 Alclad sheeting over mild-steel internal bulkheads, forming 360-degree stressed sections over driver's legs and to rear of cockpit; side boxes housing 15-gallon fuel bags draining through non-return valves into 10-gallon centre tank behind seat from whence fed to injection system

RUNNING GEAR:

Steering   Lotus rack and pinion

Front suspension   Independent with double fabricated wishbones activating inboard-mounted coil spring/damper units

Rear suspension   Independent with wishbones and two trailing links per side mounted to bulkhead in front of engine and adjustable anti-roll bar; adjustable Armstrong dampers all round

Brakes   Girling 14-4 calipers with 12-inch diameter ventilated (later solid) discs mounted on alloy wheel hubs

Wheels   Light alloy

Tyres   Crossply, Firestone 125s

DIMENSIONS AND WEIGHT:

Length   158.0 inches (4013mm)

Width   73.5 inches (1867mm)

Height   41.5 inches (1054mm)

Wheelbase   93.0 inches (2362mm)

Track   60.0 inches (1524mm) front and rear

Weight   1,124 lb (510 kg)

The Lotus 49 was basically a simple car and its monocoque body was made in L72 Alclad aluminium-alloy sheeting rivetted over steel bulkheads.

The Lotus 49 was the first car to have the Ford-Cosworth DFV V8 engine, DFV denoting "double-four-valve".

The Ford Cosworth DFV engine was designed from a clean sheet of paper. Colin Chapman and Keith Duckworth with the help of Walter Hayes, managed to persuade Harley Copp (Ford of Britain's Vice-President) that this was a good investment.

The DFV engine had a displacement of 2993 cc and a power output of 409 bhp at 9000 rpm. The DFV engine was used as a load-bearing part of the chassis (stressed member).

The Lotus 49 at Hethel on its first showing

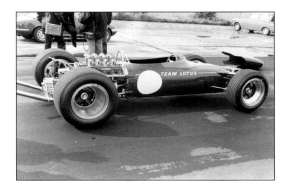

TYPE 49

GRAHAM HILL'S WORLD CHAMPIONSHIP RECORD WITH THE LOTUS 49

1967	Dutch Grand Prix	Lotus 49	Ford	Retired (camshaft gears)	1968	Mexican Grand Prix	Lotus 49B Ford	1st place
1967	Belgian Grand Prix	Lotus 49	Ford	Retired (clutch)	1969	South African Grand Prix	Lotus 49B Ford	2nd place
1967	French Grand Prix	Lotus 49	Ford	Retired (gearbox)	1969	Spanish Grand Prix	Lotus 49B Ford	Accident
1967	British Grand Prix	Lotus 49	Ford	Retired (engine)	1969	Monaco Grand Prix	Lotus 49B Ford	1st place
1967	German Grand Prix	Lotus 49	Ford	Retired (suspension)	1969	Dutch Grand Prix	Lotus 49B Ford	7th place
1967	Canadian Grand Prix	Lotus 49	Ford	4th place	1969	French Grand Prix	Lotus 49B Ford	6th place
1967	Italian Grand Prix	Lotus 49	Ford	Retired (engine)	1969	British Grand Prix	Lotus 49B Ford	7th place
1967	United States Grand Prix	Lotus 49	Ford	2nd place	1969	German Grand Prix	Lotus 49B Ford	4th place
1967	Mexican Grand Prix	Lotus 49	Ford	Retired (transmission)	1969	Italian Grand Prix	Lotus 49B Ford	Retired (driveshaft)
1968	South African Grand Prix	Lotus 49	Ford	2nd place	1969	Canadian Grand Prix	Lotus 49B Ford	Retired (camshaft)
1968	Spanish Grand Prix	Lotus 49	Ford	1st place	1969	United States Grand Prix	Lotus 49B Ford	Accident
1968	Monaco Grand Prix	Lotus 49B	Ford	1st place (pole)	1970	South African Grand Prix	Lotus 49C Ford	6th place
1968	Belgian Grand Prix	Lotus 49B	Ford	Retired (transmission)	1970	Spanish Grand Prix	Lotus 49C Ford	4th place
1968	Dutch Grand Prix	Lotus 49B	Ford	Accident	1970	Monaco Grand Prix	Lotus 49C Ford	5th place
1968	French Grand Prix	Lotus 49B	Ford	Retired (drive-shaft)	1970	Belgian Grand Prix	Lotus 49C Ford	Retired (engine)
1968	British Grand Prix	Lotus 49B	Ford	Retired (transmission)	1970	Dutch Grand Prix	Lotus 49C Ford	Not classified
1968	German Grand Prix	Lotus 49B	Ford	2nd place	1970	French Grand Prix	Lotus 49C Ford	10th place
1968	Italian Grand Prix	Lotus 49B	Ford	Lost-wheel	1970	British Grand Prix	Lotus 49C Ford	6th place
1968	Canadian Grand Prix	Lotus 49B	Ford	4th place	1970	German Grand Prix	Lotus 49C Ford	Retired (engine)
1968	United States Grand Prix	Lotus 49B	Ford	2nd place				

(above) Graham Hill at the British Grand Prix, Silverstone 16th July 1960 (right) Graham Hill in his aeroplane

Graham Hill in the Lotus 49. With the Lotus 49 Graham Hill won the 1968 Spanish Grand Prix, the 1968 Monaco Grand Prix, the 1968 Mexican Grand Prix and the 1969 Monaco Grand Prix

TYPE 49

COMPLETE RACING RECORD OF THE LOTUS 49   ENTRIES, PRACTICE TIMES AND RESULTS 1967

DATE	EVENT	CAR & CHASSIS NO.	NO.	DRIVER	PRACTICE 1	PRACTICE 2	PRACTICE 3	RACE RESULT
4 June 1967	Dutch G.P.	Lotus 49/R1	6	Graham Hill	1m 31.70s	1m 27.50s	1m 25.60s	Retired
4 June 1967	Dutch G.P.	Lotus 49/R2	5	Jim Clark	1m 28.40s	1m 27.30s	1m 26.80s	1st 2h 14m 45.10s
18 June 1967	Belgian G.P.	Lotus 49/R2	21	Jim Clark	3m 29.00s	3m 28.10s	–	6th
18 June 1967	Belgian G.P.	Lotus 49/R1	22	Graham Hill)	3m 32.90s	3m 33.40s	–	Retired
2 July 1967	French G.P.	Lotus 49/R2	6	Jim Clark	–	1m 37.50s	–	Retired
2 July 1967	French G.P.	Lotus 49/R1	7	Graham Hill	–	1m 26.20s	–	Retired
15 July 1967	British G.P.	Lotus 49/R2	5	Jim Clark	1m 27.80s	1m 26.50s	1m 26.30s	1st 1h 59m 25.60s
15 July 1967	British G.P.	Lotus 49/R1	6	Graham Hill	1m 28.70s	1m 29.20s	1m 26.00s	Retired
6 August 1967	German G.P.	Lotus 49/R1	4	Graham Hill	–	8m 31.70s	–	Retired
6 August 1967	German G.P.	Lotus 49/R2	3	Jim Clark	8m 43.40s	8m 19.80s	8m 04.10s	Retired
27 August 1967	Canadian G.P.	Lotus 49/R2	3	Jim Clark	1m 22.90s	1m 22.40s	–	Retired
27 August 1967	Canadian G.P.	Lotus 49/R1	4	Graham Hill	1m 25.00s	1m 22.70s	–	4th
27 August 1967	Canadian G.P.	Lotus 49 Ford V8	5	E. Wietzes	–	1m 30.80s	–	Retired
10 September1967	Italian G.P.	Lotus 49/R2	20	Jim Clark	1m 28.50s	1m 29.70s	–	3rd 1h 44m 08.10s
10 September1967	Italian G.P.	Lotus 49 Ford V8	22	Graham Hill	1m 29.70s	1m 30.20s	–	Retired
10 September1967	Italian G.P.	Lotus 49/R1	24	Giancarlo Baghetti	–	1m 35.20s	–	Retired
1 October 1967	United States G.P.	Lotus 49/R2	5	Jim Clark	1m 06.80s	1m 06.07s	–	1st 2h 3m 13.20s
1 October 1967	United States G.P.	Lotus 49 Ford V8	6	Graham Hill	1m 07.09s	1m 05.48s	–	2nd 2h 3m 19.50s
1 October 1967	United States G.P.	Lotus 49/R1	18	Moises Solana	–	1m 07.88s	–	Retired
22 October 1967	Mexican G.P.	Lotus 49/R1	5	Jim Clark	1m 48.97s	1m 47.56s	–	1st 1h 59m 28.70s
22 October 1967	Mexican G.P.	Lotus 49/R3	5	Graham Hill	1m 50.63s	1m 48.74s	–	Retired
22 October 1967	Mexican G.P.	Lotus 49/R2	18	Moises Solana	1m 52.86s	1m 50.52s	–	Retired

COMPLETE RACING RECORD OF THE LOTUS 49   ENTRIES, PRACTICE TIMES AND RESULTS 1968

DATE	EVENT	CAR & CHASSIS NO.	NO.	DRIVER	PRACTICE 1	PRACTICE 2	PRACTICE 3	RACE RESULT	
1st January 1968	South African G.P.	Lotus 49/R4	4	Jim Clark	1m 23.90s	1m 22.40s	1m 21.60s	1st	1h 53m 56.60s
1st January 1968	South African G.P.	Lotus 49/R3	5	Graham Hill	–	1m 24.00s	1m 22.60s	2nd	1h 54m 21.90s
12th May 1968	Spanish G.P.	Lotus 49/R1	10	Graham Hill	1m 28.40s	1m 30.60s	1m 28.70s	1st	2h 15m 20.10s
12th May 1968	Spanish G.P.	Lotus 49/R2	16	Jo Siffert	1m 30.60s	1m 30.90s	1m 29.70s	Retired	
26th May 1968	Monaco G.P.	Lotus 49B/R5	9	Graham Hill	1m 28.90s	1m 28.20s	1m 30.60s	1st	2h 00m 32.30s
26th May 1968	Monaco G.P.	Lotus 49/R1	10	Jackie Oliver	1m 31.70s	1m 35.20s	1m 33.60s	Retired	
26th May 1968	Monaco G.P.	Lotus 49/R5	17	Jo Siffert	1m 30.80s	1m 28.80s	1m 33.90s	Retired	
9th June 1968	Belgian G.P.	Lotus 49B/R5	1	Graham Hill	4m 06.10s	4m 48.10s	–	Retired	
9th June 1968	Belgian G.P.	Lotus 49B/R6	2	Jackie Oliver	–	4m 30.80s	–	5th	1h 36m 08.00s
9th June 1968	Belgian G.P.	Lotus 49/R2	3	Jo Siffert	3m 39.00	4m 36.80s	–	7th	1h 31m 48.10s
23rd June 1968	Dutch G.P.	Lotus 49B/R5	3	Graham Hill	1m 25.04s	1m 23.84s	1m 24.49s	9th, not running	
23rd June 1968	Dutch G.P.	Lotus 49B/R6	4	Jackie Oliver	1m 29.13s	1m 25.48s	1m 25.51s	Running, not classified	
23rd June 1968	Dutch G.P.	Lotus 49/R2	21	Jo Siffert	1m 26.68s	1m 25.86s	1m 27.29s	Retired	
7th July 1968	French G.P.	Lotus 49B/R5	12	Graham Hill	2m 00.00s	1m 59.10s	–	Retired	
7th July 1968	French G.P.	Lotus 49B/R6	14	Jackie Oliver	2m 02.30s	2m 00.20s	–	Did not start	
7th July 1968	French G.P.	Lotus 49/R2	34	Jo Siffert	2m 03.50s	2m 00.30 s	–	11th	2h 26m 01.30s
20th July 1968	British G.P.	Lotus 49B/R5	8	Graham Hill	1m 29.50s	1m 29.80s	1m 28.90s	Retired	
20th July 1968	British G.P.	Lotus 49/R2	9	Jackie Oliver	1m 29.90s	1m 30.70s	1m 29.40s	Retired	
20th July 1968	British G.P.	Lotus 49B/R7	22	Jo Siffert	1m 32.90s	1m 31.50s	1m 29.70s	1st	2h 01m 20.30s
4th August 1968	German G.P.	Lotus 49B/R5	3	Graham Hill	9m 46.00s	10m 14.60s	10m 36.70s	2nd	2h 23m 06.40s
4th August 1968	German G.P.	Lotus 49B/R7	16	Jo Siffert	10m 03.40s	10m 40.40s	–	Retired	
4th August 1968	German G.P.	Lotus 49B/R2	21	Jackie Oliver	–	10m 48.60s	10m 18.70s	11th	2h 21m 24.30s
8th September 1968	Italian G.P.	Lotus 49B/R6	16	Graham Hill	1m 26.57s	1m 27.90s	–	Retired	
8th September 1968	Italian G.P.	Lotus 49B/R5	19	Jackie Oliver	1m 29.80s	1m 27.40s	–	Retired	
8th September 1968	Italian G.P.	Lotus 49B/R7	20	Jo Siffert	1m 26.96s	1m 29.00s	–	Retired	
22nd September 1968	Canadian G.P.	Lotus 49B/R6	3	Graham Hill	1m 34.80s	1m 35.90s	–	4th	2h 27m 17.50s
22nd September 1968	Canadian G.P.	Lotus 49B/R2	4	Jackie Oliver	1m 36.60s	1m 35.20s	–	Retired	
22nd September 1968	Canadian G.P.	Lotus 49B/R7	12	Jo Siffert	1m 37.40s	1m 34.50s	–	Retired	
22nd September 1968	Canadian G.P.	Lotus 49B/R5	27	B. Brack	1m 42.30s	1m 41.20s	–	Retired	
6th October 1968	United States G.P.	Lotus 49B/R6	10	Graham Hill	1m 05.56s	1m 04.28s	–	2nd	1h 59m 44.97s
6th October 1968	United States G.P.	Lotus 49B/R2	11	Jackie Oliver	1m 07.46s	1m 07.86s	–	Did not start	
6th October 1968	United States G.P.	Lotus 49B/R5	12	Mario Andretti	1m 05.85s	1m 04.20s	–	Retired	
6th October 1968	United States G.P.	Lotus 49B/R7	16	Jo Siffert	1m 06.17s	1m 07.14s	–	5th	1h 59m 25.42s
3rd November 1968	Mexican G.P.	Lotus 49B/R6	10	Graham Hill	1m 46.01s	1m 46.15s	–	1st	1h 56m 43.95s
3rd November 1968	Mexican G.P.	Lotus 49B/R2	11	Jackie Oliver	1m 48.44s	1m 49.50s	–	3rd	1h 58m 24.60s
3rd November 1968	Mexican G.P.	Lotus 49B/R5	12	Moises Solana	1m 47.67s	1m 50.97s	–	Retired	
3rd November 1968	Mexican G.P.	Lotus 49B/R7	16	Jo Siffert	1m 45.52s	1m 45.22s	–	6th	1h 57m 56.26s

TYPE 49

DATE	EVENT	CAR & CHASSIS NO.	NO.	DRIVER	PRACTICE 1	PRACTICE 2	PRACTICE 3	RACE RESULT
1 March 1969	South African G.P.	Lotus 49B/R6	1	Graham Hill	1m 21.10s	1m 21.60s	1m 24.40s	2nd 1h 50m 57.90s
1 March 1969	South African G.P.	Lotus 49B/R9	2	Jochen Rindt	1m 20.70s	1m 20.20s	1m 26.60s	Retired
1 March 1969	South African G.P.	Lotus 49B/R11	3	Mario Andretti	1m 21.10s	1m 20.80s	1m 24.60s	Retired
1 March 1969	South African G.P.	Lotus 49B/R7	4	Jo Siffert	–	1m 33.10s	1m 22.20s	4th 1h 51m 28.30s
1 March 1969	South African G.P.	Lotus 49/R3	16	J. Love	1m 22.10s	1m 22.90s	–	Retired
4 May 1969	Spanish G.P.	Lotus 49B/R6	1	Graham Hill	1m 28.40s	1m 27.60s	1m 26.60s	Retired
4 May 1969	Spanish G.P.	Lotus 49B/R9	2	Jochen Rindt	1m 39.10s	1m 28.30s	1m 25.70s	Retired
4 May 1969	Spanish G.P.	Lotus 49B/R7	10	Jo Siffert	1m 30.80s	1m 30.20s	1m 28.20s	Retired
18 May 1969	Monaco G.P.	Lotus 49B/R10	1	Graham Hill	1m 25.60s	1m 25.80s	1m 25.80s	1st 1h 56m 59.40s
18 May 1969	Monaco G.P.	Lotus 49T/R8	2	R. Attwood	1m 30.60s	1m 28.00s	1m 26.50s	4th 1h 57m 52.30s
18 May 1969	Monaco G.P.	Lotus 49B/R7	9	Jo Siffert	1m 26.50s	1m 56.60s	1m 26.00s	3rd 1h 57m 34.00s
21 June 1969	Dutch G.P.	Lotus 49B/R10	1	Graham Hill	1m 22.01s	–	1m 25.13s	7th
21 June 1969	Dutch G.P.	Lotus 49B/R6	2	Jochen Rindt	1m 24.21s	1m 20.85s	1m 23.96s	Retired
21 June 1969	Dutch G.P.	Lotus 49B/R7	10	Jo Siffert	1m 26.22s	1m 23.94s	1m 24.17s	2nd 2h 07m 06.60s
6 July 1969	French G.P.	Lotus 49B/R10	1	Graham Hill	3m 15.90s	3m 09.10s	3m 05.90s	6th 1h 58m 50.60s
6 July 1969	French G.P.	Lotus 49B/R7	3	Jo Siffert	3m 09.80s	3m 06.30s	3m 06.40s	9th
6 July 1969	French G.P.	Lotus 49B/R6	15	Jochen Rindt	3m 06.40s	3m 07.00s	3m 02.50s	Retired
19 July 1969	British G.P.	Lotus 49B/R8	1	Graham Hill	–	–	1m 23.60s	7th 1h 56m 53.80s
19 July 1969	British G.P.	Lotus 49B/R6	2	Jochen Rindt	–	1m 22.39s	1m 20.80s	4th 1h 57m 04.00s
19 July 1969	British G.P.	Lotus 49B/R7	10	J Siffert	1m 23.60s	1m 24.70s	1m 22.70s	8th 1h 56m 25.80s
3 August 1969	German G.P.	Lotus 49B/R10	1	Graham Hill	8m 04.00s	8m 00.60s	7m 57.00s	4th 1h 43m 54.20s
3 August 1969	German G.P.	Lotus 49B/R6	2	Jochen Rindt	7m 58.00s	7m 54.00s	7m 48.00s	Retired
3 August 1969	German G.P.	Lotus 49B/R7	11	Jo Siffert	–	7m 50.30s	7m 55.20s	Retired
3 August 1969	German G.P.	Lotus 49B/R8	16	J. Bonnier	–	–	8m 35.00s	Retired
8 September 1969	Italian G.P.	Lotus 49B/R10	2	Graham Hill	1m 27.31s	1m 28.39s	–	9th, not running
8 September 1969	Italian G.P.	Lotus 49B/R6	4	Jochen Rindt	1m 26.43s	1m 25.48s	–	2nd 1h 39 11.34s
8 September 1969	Italian G.P.	Lotus 49B/R7	30	Jo Siffert	1m 27.29s	1m 27.04s	–	8th, not running
20 September 1969	Canadian G.P.	Lotus 49B/R10	1	Graham Hill	1m 18.60s	1m 18.30s	–	Retired
20 September 1969	Canadian G.P.	Lotus 49B/R6	2	Jochen Rindt	1m 17.90s	1m 18.00s	–	3rd 2h 00m 17.70s
20 September 1969	Canadian G.P.	Lotus 49B/R7	9	Jo Siffert	1m 18.50s	–	–	Retired
20 September 1969	Canadian G.P.	Lotus 49B/R11	25	P. Lovely	1m 25.80s	1m 22.90s	–	7th
5 October 1969	United States G.P.	Lotus 49B/R10	1	Graham Hill	1m 17.00s	1m 04.05s	–	Retired
5 October 1969	United States G.P.	Lotus 49B/R6	2	Jochen Rindt	1m 17.70s	1m 03.62s	–	1st 1h 57m 56.84s
5 October 1969	United States G.P.	Lotus 49B/R7	10	Jo Siffert	1m 18.33s	1m 04.06s	–	Retired
5 October 1969	United States G.P.	Lotus 49B/R11	21	P. Lovely	–	1m 07.55s	–	Retired
19 October 1969	Mexican G.P.	Lotus 49B/R6	2	Jochen Rindt	1m 46.00s	1m 43.94s	–	Retired
19 October 1969	Mexican G.P.	Lotus 49B/R7	10	Jo Siffert	1m 43.81s	1m 46.62s	–	Retired
19 October 1969	Mexican G.P.	Lotus 49B/R11	21	P. Lovely	–	1m 50.34s	–	9th

COMPLETE RACING RECORD OF THE LOTUS 49　　ENTRIES, PRACTICE TIMES AND RESULTS 1970

DATE	EVENT	CAR & CHASSIS NO.	NO.	DRIVER	PRACTICE 1	PRACTICE 2	PRACTICE 3	RACE RESULT
7 March 1970	South African G.P.	Lotus 49C/R6	9	Jochen Rindt	1m 20.10s	1m 20.00s	1m 19.90s	13th, not running
7 March 1970	South African G.P.	Lotus 49C/R10	10	John Miles	1m 21.50s	1m 21.40s	1m 21.00s	5th 1h 50m 36.30s
7 March 1970	South African G.P.	Lotus 49C/R7	11	Graham Hill	1m 22.00s	1m 21.60s	1m 21.70s	6th 1h 50m 46.80s
7 March 1970	South African G.P.	Lotus 49/R3	23	John Love	1m 23.20s	–	1m 23.10s	8th 1h 50m 37.30s
7 March 1970	South African G.P.	Lotus 49C/R8	25	Dave Charlton	1m 22.20s	1m 21.60s	1m 20.90s	12th, not running
19 April 1970	Spanish G.P.	Lotus 49C/R7	6	Graham Hill	1m 26.60s	1m 26.60s	1m 25.50s	4th 2h 11m 39.50s
19 April 1970	Spanish G.P.	Lotus 49C/R10	23	Alex Soler-Roig	1m 27.00s	1m 27.00s	1m 25.80s	Did not qualify
10 May 1970	Monaco G.P.	Lotus 49C/R10*	1	Graham Hill	1m 26.80s	2m 05.00s	1m 29.30s	5th
10 May 1970	Monaco G.P.	Lotus 49C/R10	2	John Miles	1m 28.70s	1.43.40s	1m 31.20s	Did not qualify
10 May 1970	Monaco G.P.	Lotus 49C/R6	3	Jochen Rindt	1m 25.90s	2.13.90s	1. 27.90s	1st 1hr 54m 36.60s
7 June 1970	Belgian G.P.	Lotus 49C/R6	20	Jochen Rindt	–	3m 30.10s	3m 32.20s	Retired
7 June 1970	Belgian G.P.	Lotus 49C/R7	23	Graham Hill	3m 50.20s	3m 38.60s	3m 37.00s	Retired
21 June 1970	Dutch G.P.	Lotus 49C/R7	15	Graham Hill	1m 23.46s	1m 21.81s	1m 21.75s	Not classified
21 June 1970	Dutch G.P.	Lotus 49B/R11	31	Pete Lovely	1m 29.11s	1m 25.88s	1m 23.37s	Did not qualify
5 July 1970	French G.P.	Lotus 49C/R7	8	Graham hill	3m 11.30s	3m 13.40s	3. 07.84s	10th
5 July 1970	French G.P.	Lotus 49C/R6	9	Alex Soler-Roig**	3m 18.78s	3m 14.49s	3m 15.71s	Did not qualify
5 July 1970	French G.P.	Lotus 49B/R11	25	Pete Lovely	5m 58.56s	3m 26.27s	3m 15.58s	Did not qualify
18 July 1970	British G.P.	Lotus 49C/R7	14	Graham Hill	1m 28.40s	1m 30.30s	–	6th
18 July 1970	British G.P.	Lotus 49C/R10	28	Emerson Fittipaldi	1m 28.10s	1m 28.30s	–	8th
18 July 1970	British G.P.	Lotus 49B/R11	29	Pete Lovely	1m 35.40s	1m 30.30s	–	Not classified
2 August 1970	German G.P.	Lotus 49C/R7	9	Graham Hill	2m 03.90s	2m 03.80s	2m 03.00s	Retired
2 August 1970	German G.P.	Lotus 49C/R10	17	Emerson Fittipaldi	2m 05.30s	2m 02.20s	2m 02.00s	4th 1h 43m 55.40s
16 August 1970	Austrian G.P.	Lotus 49C/R10	8	Emerson Fittipaldi	1m 46.10s	1m 41.86s	1m 42.00s	15th
4 October 1970	United States G.P.	Lotus 49B/R11	28	Pete Lovely	1m 07.45s	1m 08.74s	–	Did not qualify

* Hill practiced in R7, raced in Miles' car R10

** Non-starter

LOTUS 49 GRAND PRIX VICTORIES

Driven by Jimmy Clark
4 June 1967 Dutch Grand Prix
15 July 1967 1967 British Grand Prix
1 October 1967 United States Grand Prix
22 October 1967 Mexican Grand Prix
1 January 1968 South African Grand Prix

Driven by Graham Hill
12 May 1968 Spanish Grand Prix
26 May 1968 Monaco Grand Prix
3 November 1968 Mexican Grand Prix
18 May 1969 Monaco Grand Prix

Driven by Jochen Rindt
5 October 1969 United States Grand Prix
10 May 1970 Monaco Grand Prix

Driven by Jo Siffert
20 July 1968 British Grand Prix

Jim Clark also won the 1968 Tasman
Championship with the 2.5 litre Lotus 49

The last works appearance of the Lotus 49 was
on 16 August 1970 at the Austrian Grand Prix.

The Lotus Type 50 was a larger version of the Elan with more interior room and two extra small seats.

Compared to the normal Elan, the Plus 2's chassis was lengthened by twelve inches and the track widened by seven inches. The Lotus Elan +2S was introduced in October 1968. Specification was similar to the Elan +2 but with improved interior specification and "+2S" emblem on the boot.

In December 1969 the Lotus Elan +2 was discontinued but the +2S continued.

In February 1971 the Lotus Elan +2S 130 was announced with the same engine as the Elan Sprint and was identifiable by the silver roof.

In October 1972 a five speed gearbox was available as an optional extra on the Lotus Elan +2S 130. When fitted the model was identifiable by "S130/5" on the nearside rear quarter.

LOTUS TYPE 50 PLUS 2S 130/5 SPECIFICATIONS

ENGINE:
Lotus-Ford twin-cam

POWER OUTPUT:
118 bhp at 6250 rpm

GEARBOX:
Ford 4-speed/Austin Maxi 5-speed

CHASSIS:
Steel backbone with front and rear fork extensions

DIMENSIONS:

Wheelbase	8ft
Overall length	14ft
Width	5ft 3 inches
Height	3ft 11 inches
Ground clearance	4.75 inches
Kerb weight	16.75 cwt
	48% front 52% rear

A super side view of the Lotus Elan Plus Two

LOTUS ELAN RACING RECORD

DATE	EVENT	CAR NO.	DRIVERS	LAPS COMPLETED	RACE RESULT
11th August 1963	Freiburg-Schauinsland Hillclimb	23	Arthur Blank		30th
26th May 1964	Consuma Hillclimb	309	Bruno Deserti		11th
31st May 1964	Nürburgring 1000 Kms	32	Freddy Semoulin Teddy Pilette		34th
9th August 1964	Freiburg-Schauinsland Hillclimb	32	Jean-Paul Humberset		17th
30th August 1964	Swiss Mountain G.P.	120	Jean-Paul Humberset		21st
30th August 1964	Swiss Mountain G.P.	127	Charly Bonvin		25th
30th August 1964	Swiss Mountain G.P.	122	Peter Boner		32nd
30th August 1964	Swiss Mountain G.P.	123	Henri Buergisser		41st
30th August 1964	Swiss Mountain G.P.	126	Edouard Wahl		54th
11th-20th September -1964	Tour De France	141	Pierre Gele Franck Lemarque		16th
11th-20th September -1964	Tour De France	139	Henri Quernette Andre Monbaerts		Did not finish
28th February 1965	Daytona 2000 Kms	15	Lance Pruyn Newton Davis Peter Pulver	250	13th
28th February 1965	Daytona 2000 Kms	33	Fred Ashplant Harry Carter	245	17th
28th February 1965	Daytona 2000 Kms	17	Gene Parsons John W.Harden Sam Tayloe		Did not finish
16th May 1965	Spa Francorchamps	54	Mark Konig	30	15th
23rd May 1965	Nürburgring 1000 kms	92	Joachim Springer Karl Von Wendt	38	26th
23rd May 1965	Nürburgring 1000 kms	88	Georg Winkler Wolfgang Jordis	35	Not running at finish

LOTUS ELAN RACING RECORD

DATE	EVENT	CAR NO.	DRIVERS	LAPS COMPLETED	RACE RESULT
23rd May 1965	Nürburgring 1000 kms	87	Mark Konig Gabrielle Konig	24	Did not finish (Gearbox)
23rd May 1965	Nürburgring 1000 kms	90	Manfred Mohr Horst Eiteneuer	9	Did not finish (Accident)
23rd May 1965	Nürburgring 1000 kms	89	Roger Nathan Peter Taggart	5	Did not finish
13th June 1965	Rossfeld Hillclimb	38	Karl Foitek		15th
8th August 1965	Freiburg-Schauinsland Hillclimb	21	Karl Foitek		9th
8th August 1965	Freiburg-Schauinsland Hillclimb	23	Jean Paul Humberset		13th
29th August 1965	Swiss Mountain G.P.	99	Jean Paul Humberset		17th
29th August 1965	Swiss Mountain G.P.	94	Edouard Wahl		44th
29th August 1965	Swiss Mountain G.P.	93	Francois Brelaz		63rd
29th August 1965	Swiss Mountain G.P.	91	Hermann Abplanalp		69th
29th August 1965	Swiss Mountain G.P.	103	J.Peter de Meritt		Did not finish
29th August 1965	Swiss Mountain G.P.	101	Roby Joerg		Did not finish
18th September 1965	Bridgehampton Double 500	27	Fred Ashplant		3rd
5th June 1966	Nürburgring 1000 kms	69	Peter Taggart Keith Burnand	34	Not running at finish
5th June 1966	Nürburgring 1000 kms	70	Peter Mould Martin Hone	23	Not classified
5th June 1966	Nürburgring 1000 kms	78	Manfred Mohr Guenter Wallrabenstein	19	Did not finish (Engine)
5th June 1966	Nürburgring 1000 kms	72	John Hine Peter Gethin	11	Did not finish
5th June 1966	Nürburgring 1000 kms	67	Manfred Behnke Klaus Miersch	10	Did not finish
17th July 1966	Circuit of Mugello	80	James Bernard Fortman Maurizio Masini	7	35th

LOTUS ELAN RACING RECORD

DATE	EVENT	CAR NO.	DRIVERS	LAPS COMPLETED	RACE RESULT
17th July 1966	Circuit of Mugello	74	Pierre Papazian Anthony Noghes	7	36th
17th July 1966	Circuit of Mugello	77	Erminio Merlo Leonardo Duerst	2	Did not finish
17th July 1966	Circuit of Mugello	145	Andreas Eichhorn Paul Frederich	1	Did not finish
14th August 1966	Hockenheim G.P.	32	Rico Steinemann		Did not finish
14th August 1966	Hockenheim G.P.	31	Per Brandstrom		Did not finish
14th August 1966	Hockenheim G.P.	33	Andreas Eichhorn		Did not finish
28th August 1966	Swiss Mountain G.P.	221	Karl Foitek		13th
28th August 1966	Swiss Mountain G.P.	225	Hermann Buergi		27th
28th August 1966	Swiss Mountain G.P.	222	Walter Flueckiger		38th
28th August 1966	Swiss Mountain G.P.	182	Willy Elsinger		48th
28th August 1966	Swiss Mountain G.P.	227	Hermann Abplanalp		49th
28th August 1966	Swiss Mountain G.P.	223	Bernard Perrot		61st
28th August 1966	Swiss Mountain G.P.	226	Leo Krummena Cher		Did not finish
28th August 1966	Swiss Mountain G.P.	82	Hans Tschiemer		Did not finish
11th September 1966	Austrian Sports Car Grand Prix	22	Christopher St.Quintin	113	Not classified
28th May 1967	Nürburgring 1000 kms	112	Arno Gyltman Ragnar Eklund	34	22nd
28th May 1967	Nürburgring 1000 kms	111	Manfred Mohr Horst Eiteneuer	28	Did not finish
28th May 1967	Nürburgring 1000 kms	84	Harold Kroneyard Bjorn Svennson	20	Did not finish
28th May 1967	Nürburgring 1000 kms	110	Per Brandstrom Peter Trapp	12	Did not finish
23rd July 1967	Circuit of Mugello	121	Pierre Papazian	6	43rd
23rd July 1967	Circuit of Mugello	112	James Bernard Fortmann Mauro Cintolesi	3	Did not finish

LOTUS ELAN RACING RECORD

DATE	EVENT	CAR NO.	DRIVERS	LAPS COMPLETED	RACE RESULT
23rd July 1967	Circuit of Mugello	75	Willy Elsinger		Did not finish
23rd July 1967	Circuit of Mugello	68	Urs P. Dietrich Silvano Stefani	1	Did not finish
23rd July 1967	Circuit of Mugello	74	Don Marriott Bobby George		Did not finish
30th July 1967	Brands Hatch 6 Hrs	75	Peter Jackson Mike Crabtree		Not classified
30th July 1967	Brands Hatch 6 Hrs	76	Keith Burnand Peter Taggart		Not classified
20th August 1967	Austrian Sports Car Grand Prix	12	John Hine	7	Did not finish
20th August 1967	Austrian Sports Car Grand Prix	14	Don Marriott	1	Did not finish
27th August 1967	Swiss Mountain G.P.	163	Karl Foitek		12th
27th August 1967	Swiss Mountain G.P.	123	Werner Ruefenacht		19th
27th August 1967	Swiss Mountain G.P.	129	Josef Burri		37th
27th August 1967	Swiss Mountain G.P.	127	Charles H. Perenoud		40th
27th August 1967	Swiss Mountain G.P.	171	Gerhard Kobler		49th
27th August 1967	Swiss Mountain G.P.	131	Hedy Ruoss		52nd
27th August 1967	Swiss Mountain G.P.	125	"Allen"		61st
27th August 1967	Swiss Mountain G.P.	139	Richard Vogel		63rd
27th August 1967	Swiss Mountain G.P.	135	Yuan Gruaz		71st

LOTUS ELAN RACING RECORD

DATE	EVENT	CAR NO.	DRIVERS	LAPS COMPLETED	RACE RESULT
27th August 1967	Swiss Mountain G.P.	134	Jean Claude Ehinger		Did not finish
27th August 1967	Swiss Mountain G.P.	128	Hermann Burgi		Did not finish
3rd September 1967	Nürburgring 500 kms	39	James Bernard Fortmann	19	14th
3rd September 1967	Nürburgring 500 kms	31	Don Marriott	19	18th
3rd September 1967	Nürburgring 500 kms	34	Peter Jackson	18	29th
3rd September 1967	Nürburgring 500 kms	35	Per Brandstrom		Did not finish
3rd September 1967	Nürburgring 500 kms	38	Keith Burnand		Did not finish
3rd September 1967	Nürburgring 500 kms	32	Roy Adlam		Did not finish
16th May 1968	Nürburgring 1000 kms	122	Arno Gyltman Stig Johansson	34	43rd
25th April 1969	Monza 1000 kms	76	Henry Regusci Charles H. Perrenoud		Not Classified
20th March 1976	Sebring 12 Hrs	26	Armando Gonzalez Bonky Fernandez Mike Ramirez	28	Did not finish
19th March 1977	Sebring 12 Hrs	29	Bonky Fernandez Manuel Godinez Tato Ferrer	47	Did not finish
25th September 1977	Brands Hatch 6 Hrs	31	Mike Chittenden David Mercer Fred Taylor	84	15th

A super period photograph of the Lotus Elan's interior

LOTUS TYPE 51A

SPECIFICATIONS

ENGINE:
Ford Cortina GT 1600 cc cross-flow unit fitted with single downdraught Weber carburettor

GEARBOX:
Lotus modified Renault 4-speed

CHASSIS:
Multi-tubular space frame with steel undertray, fabricated bulkhead and triangulated roll-over bar

BODYWORK:
Resin bonded colour impregnated glass fibre in three sections, comprising undertray, nose section and rear engine cover

STEERING:
Rack and pinion

WHEELS:
13 inch diameter bolt on steel wheels

LOTUS 51A DIMENSIONS:

Overall length	152 inches
Overall width	59 inches
Front track	52 inches
Rear track	51.5 inches
Wheelbase	90 inches

Formula Ford was introduced in 1967 and was a formula for cars powered by the Cortina GT pushrod engine.

The Lotus Type 51 was marketed in conjunction with Motor Racing Stables driving school at Brands Hatch.

In 1968 a slightly modified model called the Lotus 51A became available. Its front suspension was by unequal length wide based wishbones with outboard spring/damper units while rear suspension was by twin radius arms, inverted wishbones and top links with outboard spring/damper units and adjustable anti-roll bar.

The Lotus 51R, displayed at the 1968 Racing Car Show, was a version of the Type 51 with cycle wings and lighting and was an attempt to turn the Type 51 into a road car.

The Type 54 was the Lotus Europa Series 2 that was launched in April 1968.

The previous bonded-on body which made repairs expensive and insurance high was redesigned on the Type 54 so that it had a detachable body like that of the Elan. Trim was also improved and electric windows were added.

The Series 2 Lotus Europa was eventually released on the home market in July 1969.

Approximately 300 Series 1 Europas were built between December 1966 and October 1967. Their chassis numbers ranged from 46/0001 with a 47 prefix for a competition version powered by the Elan twin-cam engine.

Around 350 Series 1A cars followed between October 1967 and April 1968, a number of which went to America, all having chassis numbers from 46/0300.

About 2750 Series 2 cars followed between April 1968 ad August 1971 with chassis numbers from 54/0645 and 0001P or Q. Between January 1970 and December 1971 865 further cars were built to US Federal specification. Between September 1971 and August 1972 900 Twin-cams were built in the same period.

Around 1080 Europa Specials followed between August 1972 and March 1975 on chassis numbers from 1783P and 1101Q with about 2050 Federal Europa Specials numbered from 2684R.

LOTUS TYPE 54 SPECIFICATIONS

ENGINE:
Renault 16

CAPACITY:
1470 cc (Europe and UK)
1565 cc (USA)

BORE AND STROKE:
76 mm x 81 mm (Europe and UK)
77 mm x 84 mm (U.S.A.)

TRANSMISSION:
Renault 336 4-speed Manual

FRONT SUSPENSION:
Independent by wishbone and coil spring, anti-roll bar

REAR SUSPENSION:
Independent by trailing radius arms, links, coil spring/damper units

CHASSIS:
Steel box section backbone

TYPE 54 DIMENSIONS:

Length	13ft 1 inch
Width	5ft 4.5 inches
Height	3ft 7 inches
Wheelbase	7ft 7 inches
Kerb weight	1450 lb

LOTUS TYPE 56 SPECIFICATIONS

ENGINE:
Pratt & Whitney STN6B-74 gas turbine with 3-stage axial compressor

TRANSMISSION:
Engine output shaft coupled directly to Ferguson transfer drive. ZF spiral-bevel final drive units front and rear

FRONT SUSPENSION:
Fabricated unequal length upper and lower wishbones, inboard coil/spring damper

REAR SUSPENSION:
Fabricated unequal length upper and lower wishbones. Lower wishbone is a different design compared to the front suspension

The Lotus Type 56 was the four wheel drive, gas turbine car used for the Indianapolis 500 Mile Race in 1968. It was sponsored by Andy Granatelli and his STP Company.

Four cars were built in 1968, and these were chassis "56/1" (Indianapolis race number 60), chassis "56/2" (Indianapolis race number 30), chassis "56/3" (Indianapolis race number 70) and chassis "56/4" (race number 20).

Following the death of Mike Spence during qualifying only Jo Leonard, Art Pollard and Graham Hill drove the cars in the 1968 Indianapolis race.

Some believe that chassis "56/2" that crashed in practice became the unique "56B/1".

DIMENSIONS:

Wheelbase	8ft 6 inches
Overall height	2ft 8 inches
Overall length	14ft 2 inches
Ground clearance	3.5 inches
Weight	1350 lbs
Weight distribution	43% front 57% rear

Graham Hill's car chassis "56/3" had race number 70
The STP-Lotus crew are in the background

On the Lotus 56 the power unit was offset two inches to the right to accomodate front and rear propeller shafts that passed along the left side of the tube.

This publicity photograph shows Parnelli Jones in STP's Wallis-built "Silent Sam" Turbocar and Jim Clark in the Lotus 56. Beside them are Andy Granatelli and Colin Chapman

TYPE 56B

Colin Chapman and Emerson Fittipaldi in the Lotus 56B

THE RACING RECORD OF CHASSIS 56B/1

DATE	EVENT	CIRCUIT	DRIVER	PRACTICE 1	PRACTICE 2	PRACTICE 3	RACE RESULT
21 March 1971	Race of Champions	Brands Hatch	Emerson Fittipaldi	–	–	–	Retired, suspension
9 April 1971	Rothmans Int Trophy	Oulton Park	Reine Wisell	–	–	–	Retired, suspension
8 May 1971	International Trophy	Silverstone	Emerson Fittipaldi	–	–	–	Running, not classified
13 June 1971	Jochen Rindt Memorial	Hockenheim	Dave Walker	–	–	–	–
20 June 1971	Dutch Grand Prix	Zandvoort	Dave Walker	–	1m 42.57s	1m 21.83s	Accident
17 July 1971	British Grand Prix	Silverstone	Reine Wisell	1m 22.684s	1m 22.38s	1m 20.80s	13th place
5 September 1971	Italian Grand Prix	Monza	Emerson Fittipaldi	1m 29.18s	1m 26.09s	1m 25.18s	8th place
12 September 1971	Preis der Nationen	Hockenheim	Emerson Fittipaldi	–	–	–	2nd place

On the Lotus 56B engine life was measured in hours, not miles. Other drivers of this car apart from Emerson Fittipaldi, were Reine Wisell and Dave Walker. The car had made its debut in the Race of Champions at Brands Hatch on the 21st March 1971 where Emerson Fittipaldi was forced to retire with suspension failure. Its last appearance, again in the hands of Emerson Fittipaldi, was at Hockenheim for the Preis der Nationen on the 12th September 1971. Fittipaldi finished second in this F5000 event.

The Lotus Type 59 was designed by Dave Baldwin and it was distinguishable by the unusual twin-nostril air intakes at the front. Rolf Stommelen can be seen removing his crash helmet after taking the chequered flag at the 1969 German Grand Prix with his Lotus 59B ablaze. Emerson Fittipaldi set the fastest lap times at Brands Hatch, Crystal Palace and Mallory Park in 1969 with the Lotus 59 in F3 events. Other drivers of these models apart from Rolf Stommelen, were John Miles, Roy Pike, Alan Rollinson, Graham Hill, Jochen Rindt and Emerson Fittipaldi.

LOTUS TYPE 57 and 58 SPECIFICATIONS

ENGINE:
Ford Cosworth DFW and Cosworth FVA

CUBIC CAPACITY:
2498 cc and 1598 cc

TRANSMISSION:
ZF 5D512/Hewland FT200

DIMENSIONS:

Length	12ft 8 inches
Width	5ft 10 inches
Height	2ft 7 inches

LOTUS TYPE 59 and 59B SPECIFICATIONS

ENGINE:
Holbay Ford R68

TRANSMISSION
Hewland 5-speed or Hewland FT200

CHASSIS:
Multi-tubular space-frame with square section tubing

DIMENSIONS:

Wheelbase	7ft 8.75 inches
Track	4ft 8 inches

LOTUS SEVEN SERIES IV SPECIFICATIONS OF THE TYPE 60

ENGINE:

Type	4 in-line, water-cooled cast iron block and aluminium head
Bore and stroke	3.25 x 2.86 inches (82.5 x 72.6mm)
Valve gear	Chain driven twin overhead cams
Compression ratio	9.5 to 1

FRONT SUSPENSION:
Independent unequal length control arms, coil springs, anti-sway bar

REAR SUSPENSION:
Rigid axle, lower trailing arms, upper trailing arms, coil springs

STEERING:
Rack and pinion

DIMENSIONS:

Wheelbase	91 inches
Front track	48.8 inches
Rear track	51.5 inches
Length	146.3 inches
Width	60.5 inches
Height	44.0 inches
Ground clearance	6.5 inches

LOTUS TYPE 60 PERFORMANCE

0 to 30 mph	2.6 seconds
0 to 40 mph	4.2 seconds
0 to 50 mph	6.0 seconds
0 to 60 mph	8.7 seconds
0 to 70 mph	11.4 seconds
Standing quarter mile	15.8 seconds @ 82.4 mph

The Lotus Seven Series 4 was first seen by the public at the Geneva Motor Show of 1970 and had been aimed at at different market to its predecessors.

Mike Warner who had been a Group Purchasing Manager at Lotus was to redesign the Lotus Seven and was assisted by Alan Barrett and Peter Lucas.

The car boasted a top speed of 116 mph and was produced from late 1969 to the latter part of 1972. The Lotus Seven Series 4 continued for about a year as the Caterham Seven, and this was eventually replaced by the Caterham Super Seven. A variety of engines were available for the Type 60 and included the Ford 1600, the Lotus Twin Cam and the Holbay Big Valve Twin Cam.

Top speed of the Lotus Seven Type 60 differed slightly according to which engine choice was made. The very last Lotus Seven Series 4 cars left Lotus in October 1972.

TYPE 61 AND 61M

The Lotus Type 61 was first seen at the 1969 Racing Car Show, and was powered by the Lotus-Holbay LH105 engine which was capable of developed 105 bhp.

The car's front suspension consisted of unequal length wishbones located by nylon bushes, outboard springs with adjustable platforms and Armstrong adjustable damper units.

The rear suspension was by lower wishbones, top links and radius arms mounted on adjustable spherical bearings and nylon, bushes, outboard springs with adjustable platforms, and Armstrong damper units.

The car achieved success in the hands of the Jim Russell Racing School and it won the Les Leston Formula Ford Championship. A total of 248 cars were made.

LOTUS TYPE 61 SPECIFICATIONS

ENGINE:
Lotus-Holbay LH105 Ford Cortina 1599 cc pushrod

GEARBOX:
Hewland MarkVI four speed and reverse close ratio

CHASSIS:
Multi-tubular space frame constructed of round 1 square section tube with steel under tray

DIMENSIONS:

Wheelbase	7ft 6 inches
Overall length	12ft 6 inches
Ground clearance	3.75 inches
Overall height	3ft 3 inches
Overall width	4ft 11 inches

BRAKES
Girling hydraulic with 9 inch front and 9.5 inch rear discs and cast iron calipers

STEERING:
Light-weight rack and pinion

LOTUS TYPE 61

WHEELS AND TYRES

Front	5.5J x 13 pressed steel fitted with 16.5 x 13 Firestone F100
Rear	5.5J x 13 pressed steel fitted with 185 x 13 Firestone F100

1.5 inch alloy wheel spacers front and rear

EMERSON FITTIPALDI'S RACING RECORD WITH THE LOTUS 61M

1st February 1979	BUAFF Championship	Heat 1	Rio
1st February 1979	BUAFF Championship	Heat 2	Rio
1st February 1979	BUAFF Championship	Heat Aggregate	Rio
8th February 1979	BUAFF Championship	Heat 1	Curitiba
8th February 1979	BUAFF Championship	Heat 2	Curitiba
8th February 1979	BUAFF Championship	Heat Aggregate	Curitiba
15th February 1979	BUAFF Championship	Heat 1	Forteleza
15th February 1979	BUAFF Championship	Heat 2	Forteleza
15th February 1979	BUAFF Championship	Heat Aggregate	Forteleza
22nd February 1979	BUAFF Championship	Heat 1	Rio
22nd February 1979	BUAFF Championship	Heat 2	Rio
22nd February 1979	BUAFF Championship	Heat Aggregate	Rio
29th February 1979	BUAFF Championship	Heat 1	Interlagos
29th February 1979	BUAFF Championship	Heat 2	Interlagos
29th February 1979	BUAFF Championship	Heat Aggregate	Interlagos

Only two Lotus Type 62s were made, and they were raced by Gold Leaf Team Lotus in 1969. Although entered as Lotus Europas, the car in fact had a tubular space-frame instead of a backbone chassis. The car had been designed by Martin Wade and was distinguishable by its rounded tail and wheel arches for Formula 1 wheels and tyres. The car first appeared at the 1969 BOAC race at Brands Hatch where John Miles and Brian Muir drove it into 13th place and won the two-litre Prototype class. In the Trophy of the Dunes, Zandvoort, the cars these two cars came to gain fourth place and sixth place. The cars were not raced after 1969 by Lotus, and one of the cars was eventually sold to jazz band leader Chris Barber.

LOTUS TYPE 62 SPECIFICIATIONS

ENGINE:
Lotus LV 220

GEARBOX:
ZF 5DS12

CHASSIS:
Multi-tubular space-frame

PRODUCTION:
2 cars

DIMENSIONS:

Wheelbase	7ft 7 inches
Front track	4ft 4 inches
Rear track	4ft 4 inches
Overall length	12ft 10 inches

The Lotus Type 63 drew on Lotus' previous experience with four-wheel-drive racing cars, such as the STP Turbine Car of 1967.

It was a monocoque, with its engine turned around 180°. The clutch and five-speed Hewland gearbox were ahead of the engine. Driveshafts carry the power to front and rear differentials in 42% and 58% proportions.

John Miles managed to achieve an unofficial 1 minute 23.3 second lap in practice before the British Grand Prix and finished tenth in the race itself.

Jochen Rindt and John Miles drove the Lotus 63, but without much success, though Rindt gained second place in the Gold Cup race at Oulton Park on the 16th August 1969. Jochen Rindt said of the Lotus 63 "You just can't 'race' the car".

LOTUS TYPE 63 SPECIFICATIONS

ENGINE:
Ford Cosworth DFV

GEARBOX:
Lotus-Hewland 5-speed gearbox with four-wheel drive

CHASSIS:
18 swg aluminium monocoque

FRONT AND REAR SUSPENSION:
Fabricated double wishbone, and vertical coil spring damper units

TYPE 64

For 1969, Colin Chapman built four new STP-Lotus wedge design racers, powered by turbo charged Ford V8 racing engines.

Chassis 64/1 was a spare care for the 1969 Indianapolis 500 and had race entry number "60".

Chassis 64/2 which had Indianapolis race entry number "70" was the car that would have been assigned to Graham Hill.

Chassis 64/3 which had Indianapolis race entry number "80" was the car that would have been assigned to Austrian Jochen Rindt who signed for Lotus in 1969.

Chassis 64/4 which had Indianapolis race entry number "2" was the car to have been assigned to Mario Andretti. Andretti crashed heavily following the failure of a rear right hub, and the car was written off.

Because of insufficient time for new hubs to be made and tested the cars were withdrawn from the race. This was the last appearance of Lotus at the Indianapolis race.

LOTUS TYPE 64 SPECIFICATIONS

ENGINE:
Ford Quad-cam V8 alloy with turbocharger and Hilborn fuel injection

CUBIC CAPACITY:
2605 cc

POWER OUTPUT:
Over 700 bhp at 10,000 rpm

TRANSMISSION:
Lotus-designed ZF and Hewland-made four wheel drive system

FRONT SUSPENSION:
Fabricated unequal-length upper and lower wishbones

REAR SUSPENSION:
Fabricated unequal-length upper and lower wishbones. Lower wishbone of a different design to the front suspension

DIMENSIONS:
Wheelbase	100 inches
Overall length	160 inches
Overall width	75 inches
Overall height	32 inches
Weight	1400 lbs
Weight distribution	47% front 53% rear

In practice on Tuesday, 13th May Graham Hill reached 161.8 mph while Mario Andretti reached 171.5 mph.

Mario Andretti's practice crash and the subsequent withdrawal of the cars from the competition resulted in a dispute about the STP purchase of the cars. STP claimed they had not established their ability to run in competition which had been a pre-condition of purchase.

Even in the past three years the sale of cars and spares to Andy Granatelli had been difficult. Following the Indy practice crash Andy Granatelli had agreed to buy them for ninety-five thousand dollars but at a meeting between STP and Lotus, Colin Chapman walked out over the price of spares and refused to sell the cars. Andrew Ferguson hid the cars so STP would find it difficult to do anything about them and he had arranged for Ford engines to be taken out and returned to Ford. Andrew Ferguson had managed to use the home garage of Lotus's shipping agents secretary. Mechanics Dale Porteous, Arthur Birchall and Hywel Absalom helped with the task. The cars eventually came back to England.

TYPE 69 AND 69F

Changes to Formula 2 regulations in 1970 made the use of bag-type fuel tanks compulsory and many cars required substantial modification.

Jochen Rindt formed his own team, Jochen Rindt Racing Limited which was administered by Bernie Ecclestone to race the works Lotus 69s. Rindt won four races including Thruxton (57m 41.00s), Nürburgring (1h 23m 54.70s), Pau (1h 33m 37.60s) and Zolder (1h 10m 50.80s). Emerson Fittipaldi came second at the Imola Grand Prix in a Lotus 69.

Another version of the Lotus 69, the Lotus 69F, was used for Formula Ford. This car had narrower wheels and a chisel nose and enjoyed much success in the hands of drivers such as Neil Ginn, Graham Cuthbert, John Sheldon and Peter Harrington.

LOTUS 69 RACING SUCCESSES

EVENT	DATE	CAR	DRIVER	POS	TIME
Teretonga International	24th January 1971	Lotus 69-Waggott	Leo Geoghegan	6th place	–
Jim Clark Trophy	4th April 1971	Lotus 69-Ford FVA	Gerry Birrell	6th place	1h 28m 36.10s
Jochen Rindt Memorial Trophy Race	12th April 1971	Lotus 69-Ford FVA	Wilson Fittipaldi	6th place	1 h 03m 37.60s
Nürburgring	2nd May 1971	Lotus 69-Ford FVA	Emerson Fittipaldi	2nd place	1h 20m 37.00s
Madrid Grand Prix	16th May 1971	Lotus 69-Ford FVA	Emerson Fittipaldi	1st place	1h 29m 42.90s
Madrid Grand Prix	16th May 1971	Lotus 69-Ford FVA	Wilson Fittipaldi	6th place	1h 30m 42.90s
Hilton Transport Trophy	31st May 1971	Lotus 69-Ford FVA	Emerson Fittipaldi	1st place	0h 42m 03.00s
Hilton Transport Trophy	31st May 1971	Lotus 69-Ford FVA	Gerry Birrell	6th place	–
Roven Grand Prix	27th June 1971	Lotus 69-Ford FVA	Francois Migault	5th place	0h 56m 41.80s
Mantorp Grand Prix	8th August 1971	Lotus 69-Ford FVA	Gerry Birrell	6th place	1h 47m 57.70s
Albi Grand Prix	26th September 1971	Lotus 69-Ford FVA	Emerson Fittipaldi	1st place	1h 16m 49.10s
Rome Grand Prix	10th October 1971	Lotus 69-Ford FVA	Gerry Birrell	5th place	1h 27m 07.70s
Jochen Rindt Memorial Trophy Race	11th June 1972	Lotus 69-Ford	Emerson Fittipaldi	1st place	1h 13m 39.20s
Roven-Les-Essarts Grand Prix	25th June 1972	Lotus 69-Ford	Emerson Fittipaldi	1st place	0h 54m 20.00s
Jochen Rindt Memorial Trophy Race	9th July 1972	Lotus 69-Ford	Emerson Fittipaldi	1st place	0h 59m 23.51s
Formula 2 Torneio, Brazil	29th October 1972	Lotus 69-Ford	Emerson Fittipaldi	1st place	1h 15m 43.54s
Formula 2 Torneio, Brazil	5th November 1972	Lotus 69-Ford	Emerson Fittipaldi	2nd place	1h 14m 49.10s
Winfield Teretonga International	30th January 1972	Lotus 69-Ford FVC	Ken Smith	7th place	–
Forward Trust Championship Race	12th March 1972	Lotus 69-Ford	Barrie Maskell	1st place	0h 16m 12.00s
Forward Trust Championship Race	12th March 1972	Lotus 69-Ford	Geddes Yeates	3rd place	–
Shell British Championship Race	31st March 1972	Lotus 69-Ford	Barrie Maskell	3rd place	0h 33m 57.00s
Shell British Championship Race	31st March 1972	Lotus 69-Ford	Bengt Radmyr	9th place	–
Shell British Championship Race	31st March 1972	Lotus 69-Ford	Barrie Maskell	2nd place	0h 31m 47.60s
Zandvoort Netherlands	30th April 1972	Lotus 69-Ford	Roger Keele	8th place	–
Agip Cup Monza Grand Prix Circuit	24th September 1972	Lotus 69-Ford	Eltore Ricci	5th place	–
15th Formula 3 Monaco Grand Prix	2nd June 1973	Lotus 69-Ford	Gaudenzio Mantova	7th place	–
Polifac Formel 3 Trophy Rennen	26th May 1974	Lotus 69-Ford	Josef Kremer	5th place	–

LOTUS TYPE 69 SPECIFICATIONS FOR FORMULA TWO

ENGINE:
1600 cc twin overhead camshaft. Fuel injection Cosworth FVA dry sump lubrication with remote oil tank mounted at rear of chassis

TRANSMISSION:
Hewland FT200 five speed and reverse close ratio gearbox. Driven through a Borg and Beck clutch with 9/31 crown wheel and pinion and drive shafts fitted with self centring devices.

FRONT SUSPENSION:
Independent by unequal length wide based wishbones located by adjustable spherical bearings. Adjustable outboard spring/damper units located by spherical bearings. Adjustable anti-roll bar

REAR SUSPENSION:
Independent by longer wishbones, top links and radius arms mounted on adjustable spherical bearings, adjustable outboard spring/damper units located by spherical bearings and adjustable anti-roll bars

DIMENSIONS:

Wheelbase	93 inches
Front track	55 inches
Rear track	56 inches
Ground clearance	4.25 inches (f)
	4.5 inches (r)

TYPE 70

Design of the Lotus Type 70 for 1970 was given to Martin Wade of Lotus Components. His brief, according to Autosport Magazine at the time, was to come up with a fairly simple, clean-looking car which could be run by the average racing mechanic in any part of the world and which could take a variety of engines.

The Lotus Type 70 had two side boxes in 16 swg BA21 aluminium, joined by an 18 swg L72 aluminium undertray. The inner skins of the monocoque were also made in 18 swg L72.

The cars first appearance was at Sebring where it was driven by Mario Andretti and was entered by a team new to racing, Koshland Competition, which was a consortium of New York businessman headed by Tony Koshland.

The car was also entered in the 1971 Tasman Series and was fourth at Levin when driven by David Oxton, second at Warwich Farm when driven by Chris Amon and fourth at Sandown Park when driven by Chris Amon.

LOTUS TYPE 70 SPECIFICATIONS

ENGINE:
Ford Boss V8

CUBIC CAPACITY:
4945 cc

POWER OUTPUT:
480 bhp

GEARBOX:
Hewland LG600 5-speed

CARBURATION:
Four 48IDA downdraught Webers

LOTUS TYPE 70 SUSPENSION

FRONT SUSPENSION:
Front suspension is mounted on an 18 swg mild steel box section arrangement rivetted to the front of the monocoque. The top tubes bifurcate at their other ends to provide a mounting for the wishbones and coil spring/damper units. The double wishbone layout uses half-pressings that are seam welded together to form strong, light wishbones

REAR SUSPENSION:
Rear suspension is mounted on a tripod type of steel sub-frame which locates on the engine bellhousing and the rear of the gearbox. A dural beam is bolted below the box and and aluminium plate is bolted to the rear of the box to take suspension loads.

At the Levin International on 2 January 1971 David Oxton's 4th place took 51m 10.40s while at the Rothmans 100 International on 14 February 1971 Chris Amon's 2nd place took 65m 28.80s

TYPE 72

At the time of the Grand Prix at Zandvoort in 1970, Jochen Rindt's Lotus 72 had been much modified to eliminate anti-drive and anti-squat and he was able to score a win.

He won again at Clermont Ferrand and snatched a third victory at Brands Hatch when Brabham ran out of fuel on the final lap. Jochen Rindt won again with the Lotus 72 at Hockenheim. Rindt was killed during practice at Monza, the cause being either failure of a front brake shaft or the fact that the car was out of control aerodynamically as it had been seen fish tailing.

Aerodynamic instability on cold tyres and running without nose wings or aerofoil were significant factors. By 1976 after much legal argument, Colin Chapman was cleared of all claims regarding Rindt's death. The Italian authorities acknowledged that it was an incorrectly fitted guard rail that caused Rindt's death. The guard rail had allowed the front of the car to go under it instead of deflecting it, causing a much more violent impact.

In consequence Lotus did not attend the Italian Grand Prix nor the Canadian Grand Prix. Graham Hill was sole Lotus representative at the Canadian Grand Prix in Rob Walker's 72/R4 and finished unclassified.

By September 1970, Lotus decided they would enter Watkins Glen. John Miles was no longer used, replaced by Reine Wisell who took over 72/R3.

When Jacky Ickx, the only other contender for the 1970 World Championship came only fourth at Watkins Glen and Fittipaldi won the race, Rindt became officially the 1970 World Champion. Rindt was the first ever posthumous winner of the World Championship title.

Jochen Rindt (above) had won the 1965 Le Mans 24 Hrs with Masten Gregory in a Ferrari 250 LM and drove for Brabham during the 1968 season. Rindt's first victory in the Lotus 72 came at the 1970 Dutch Grand Prix. It was a sad victory as Piers Courage was killed in a crash. John Rindt and Nina Rindt were friends of Piers Courage and Sally Courage and Rindt discussed retiring with Ecclestone. Rindt decided to continue but told Chapman he would retire if he won the 1970 World Championship.

COMPLETE CHAMPIONSHIP RACING RECORD OF THE LOTUS 72 ENTRIES, PRACTICE TIMES AND RESULTS 1970

DATE	EVENT	CAR & CHASSIS NO.	NO.	DRIVER	PRACTICE 1	PRACTICE 2	PRACTICE 3	RACE RESULT	
19 April 1970	Spanish G.P.	Lotus 72/R2	3	Jochen Rindt	1m 24.80s	1m 24.80s	1m 24.80s	Retired	
19 April 1970	Spanish G.P.	Lotus 72/R1	19	John Miles	1m 25.90s	1m 25.90s	1m 25.30s	Non Starter	
10 May 1970	Monaco G.P.	Lotus 72/R	2T	John Miles	–	–	1m 31.20s	Non Starter	
7 June 1970	Belgian G.P.	Lotus 72/R1	21	John Miles	3m 40.10s	3m 40.70s	3m 33.80s	Retired	
7 June 1970	Belgian G.P.	Lotus 72/R2	22	Alex Soler-Roig	–	–	–	Non Starter	
21 June 1970	Dutch G.P.	Lotus 72/R2	10	Jochen Rindt	1m 19.48s	1m 19.73s	1m 18.50s	1st	1h 50m 43.41s
21 June 1970	Dutch G.P.	Lotus 72/R1	12	John Miles	1m 22.96s	1m 21.22s	1m 20.24s	7th	
5 July 1970	French G.P.	Lotus 72/R2	6	Jochen Rindt	3m 05.04s	3m 00.74s	2m 59.74s	1st	1h 55m 57.00s
5 July 1970	French G.P.	Lotus 72/R1	7	John Miles	3m 07.31s	3m 04.37s	3m 04.16s	8th	1h 58m 44.17s
18 July 1970	British G.P.	Lotus 72/R2	5	Jochen Rindt	1m 24.80s	1m 26.30s	–	1st	1h 57m 02.00s
18 July 1970	British G.P.	Lotus 72/R1	6	John Miles	1m 26.80s	1m 25.90s	–	Retired	
2 August 1970	German G.P.	Lotus 72/R2	2	Jochen Rindt	2m 01.60s	8m 59.70s	2m 01.50s	1st	1h 42m 00.30s
2 August 1970	German G.P.	Lotus 72/R3	16	John Miles	2m 03.80s	2m 01.60s	2m 02.30s	Retired	
16 August 1970	Austrian G.P.	Lotus 72/R2	6	Jochen Rindt	1m 41.60s	1m 39.23s	1m 59.20s	Retired	
16 August 1970	Austrian G.P.	Lotus 72/R3	7	John Miles	1m 42.90s	1m 43.80s	1m 41.46s	Retired	
6 September 1970	Italian G.P.	Lotus 72/R2	22	Jochen Rindt	1m 29.97s	1m 25.71s	1m 26.75s	Fatal Accident	
6 September 1970	Italian G.P.	Lotus 72/R3	24	John Miles	1m 28.54s	1m 26.51s	–	Withdrawn	
6 September 1970	Italian G.P.	Lotus 72/R5	26	Emerson Fittipaldi	–	1m 28.39s	–	Practice Accident	
6 September 1970	Italian G.P.	Lotus 72/R4	28	Graham Hill	1m 26.38s	1m 28.66s	1m 32.02s	Withdrawn	
20 September 1970	Canadian G.P.	Lotus 72/R4	9	Graham Hill	–	1m 35.80s	1m 39.30s	Unclassified	
4 October 1970	United States G.P.	Lotus 72/R4	14	Graham Hill	1m 04.81s	1m 05.24s	–	Retired	
4 October 1970	United States G.P.	Lotus 72/R3	23	Reine Wisell	1m 05.58s	1m 04.79s	–	3rd	1h 58m 17.96s
4 October 1970	United States G.P.	Lotus 72/R5	24	Emerson Fittipaldi	1m 04.69s	1m 03.67s	–	1st	1h 57m 32.79s
25 October 1970	Mexican G.P.	Lotus 72/R4	14	Graham Hill	1m 46.35s	1m 44.13s	–	Retired	
25 October 1970	Mexican G.P.	Lotus 72/R3	23	Reine Wisell	1m 45.07s	1m 44.59s	–	Unclassified	
25 October 1970	Mexican G.P.	Lotus 72/R5	24	Emerson Fittipaldi	1m 48.13s	1m 48.60s	–	Retired	

Type 72

Jochin Rindt came first in the Dutch Grand Prix, British Grand Prix, French Grand Prix and German Grand Prix in 1970. Opposite page shows Rindt was top of the World Championship of Drivers in 1970

RESULTS OF THE WORLD CHAMPIONSHIP 1970

POS.	DRIVER	S.AFRICA	SPAIN	MONACO	BELGIUM	HOLLAND	FRANCE	G.B.	GERMANY	AUSTRIA	ITALY	CANADA	USA	MEXICO	TOTAL
1.	Jochen Rindt	–	–	9	–	9	9	9	9	–	–	–	–	–	45
2.	Jacky Ickx	–	–	–	–	4	–	–	6	9	–	9	3	9	40
3.	Clay Regazzoni	–	–	–	–	3	–	3	–	6	9	6	–	6	33
4.	Denis Hulme	6	–	3	–	–	3	4	4	–	3	–	–	4	27
5.	Jack Brabham	9	–	6	–	–	4	6	–	–	–	–	–	–	25
5.	Jackie Stewart	4	9	–	–	6	–	–	–	–	6	–	–	–	25
7.	Pedro Rodriguez	–	–	1	9	–	–	–	–	3	–	3	6	1	23
7.	Chris Amon	–	–	–	6	–	6	2	–	–	–	4	2	2	23
9.	Jean-Pierre Beltoise	3	–	–	4	2	–	–	–	1	4	–	–	3	16
10.	Emerson Fittipaldi	–	–	–	–	–	–	–	3	–	–	–	9	–	12
11.	Rolf Stommelen	–	–	–	2	–	–	–	2	4	2	–	–	–	10
12.	Henri Pescarolo	–	–	4	1	–	2	–	1	–	–	–	–	–	8
13.	Graham Hill	1	3	2	–	–	–	1	–	–	–	–	–	–	7
14.	Bruce McLaren	–	6	–	–	–	–	–	–	–	–	–	–	–	6
15.	Mario Andretti	–	4	–	–	–	–	–	–	–	–	–	–	–	4
15	Reine Wisell	–	–	–	–	–	–	–	–	–	–	–	4	–	4
17.	Ignazio Giunti	–	–	–	3	–	–	–	–	–	–	–	–	–	3
17.	John Surtees	–	–	–	–	1	–	–	–	–	–	2	–	–	3
19.	John Miles	2	–	–	–	–	–	–	–	–	–	–	–	–	2
19.	Johnny Servoz-Gavin	–	2	–	–	–	–	–	–	–	–	–	–	–	2
19.	Jackie Oliver	–	–	–	–	–	–	–	–	2	–	–	–	–	2
22.	Dan Gurney	–	–	–	–	–	1	–	–	–	–	–	–	–	1
22.	Francois Cevert	–	–	–	–	–	–	–	–	–	–	1	–	–	1
22.	Peter Gethin	–	–	–	–	–	–	–	–	–	–	1	–	–	1
22.	Derek Bell	–	–	–	–	–	–	–	–	–	–	–	1	–	1

CONSTRUCTORS' CUP

POS.	MANUFACTURER														
1.	Lotus-Ford	2	3	9	–	9	9	9	9	–	–	–	9	–	59
2.	Ferrari	–	–	–	3	4	–	3	6	9	9	9	3	9	52
3.	March-Ford	4	9	–	6	6	6	2	–	–	6	4	2	3	48
4.	Brabham Ford	9	–	6	2	–	4	6	2	4	2	–	–	–	35
4.	McLaren-Ford	6	6	3	–	1	3	4	4	–	3	1	–	4	35
6.	BRM	–	–	1	9	–	–	–	–	3	–	3	6	1	23
6.	Matra-Simca	3	–	4	4	2	2	–	1	1	4	–	–	2	23
8.	Surtees-Ford	–	–	–	–	–	–	–	–	–	–	2	1	–	3

Jochen Rindt is highest placed World Championship driver with 45 points in 1970, while Lotus-Ford lead the Constructors' Cup.

Type 72

Despite having won the World Championship in 1970, Lotus did not win one race in 1971 at Championship level. Dave Charlton came first in a few South African races, the 25th Anniversary Trophy on the 7th August 1971, the Rand Spring Trophy on the 9th October 1971 and the Welkon 100 on the 23rd October 1971. At the Monaco Grand Prix of 1971 Fittipaldi was fifth and Wisell retired with a collapsed hub bearing. Fittipaldi missed the Dutch Grand Prix due to a road accident. His place was taken by Dave Walker who crashed a Lotus 72 in practice and crashed the Lotus 56B on lap six in the race. At the Austrian Grand Prix things looked up when Fittipaldi was second and Wisell was fourth.

RESULTS OF THE WORLD CHAMPIONSHIP 1971

POS	DRIVER	S.AFRICA	SPAIN	MONACO	HOLLAND	FRANCE	G.B.	GERMANY	AUSTRIA	ITALY	CANADA	USA	TOTAL
1.	Jackie Stewart	6	9	9	–	9	9	9	–	–	9	2	62
2.	Ronnie Peterson	–	–	6	3	–	6	2	–	6	6	4	33
3.	Francois Cevert	–	–	–	–	6	–	6	–	4	1	9	26
4.	Jacky Ickx	–	6	4	9	–	–	–	–	–	–	–	19
4.	Jo Siffert	–	–	–	1	3	–	–	9	–	–	6	19
6.	Emerson Fittipaldi	–	–	2	–	4	4	–	6	–	–	–	16
7.	Clay Regazzoni	4	–	–	4	–	–	4	–	–	–	1	13
8.	Mario Andretti	9	–	–	–	–	–	3	–	–	–	–	12
9.	Reine Wisell	3	–	–	–	1	–	–	3	–	2	–	9
9.	Chris Amon	2	4	–	–	2	–	–	–	1	–	–	9
9.	Denis Hulme	1	2	3	–	–	–	–	–	–	3	–	9
9.	Pedro Rodriguez	–	3	–	6	–	–	–	–	–	–	–	9
9.	Peter Gethin	–	–	–	–	–	–	–	–	9	–	–	9
14.	Tim Schenken	–	–	–	–	–	–	1	4	–	–	–	5
14.	Howden Ganley	–	–	–	–	–	–	–	–	2	–	3	5
16.	Henri Pescarolo	–	–	–	–	–	3	–	1	–	–	–	4
16.	Mark Donohue	–	–	–	–	–	–	–	–	–	4	–	4
18.	Rolf Stommelen	–	–	1	–	–	2	–	–	–	–	–	3
18.	John Surtees	–	–	–	2	–	1	–	–	–	–	–	3
18.	Mike Hailwood	–	–	–	–	–	–	–	–	–	3	–	3
21.	Graham Hill	–	–	–	–	–	–	–	2	–	–	–	2
22.	Jean-Pierre Beltoise	–	1	–	–	–	–	–	–	–	–	–	1

LOTUS 72D-FORD SPECIFICATIONS

ENGINE:
Cosworth - Ford DFV

BORE AND STROKE:
85.6 mm x 64.8 mm

CAPACITY:
2993 cc

COMPRESSION:
11 to 1

MAXIMUM POWER AND RPM:
440 at 10000

VALVE SIZES:
1.32 inches x 2

VALVE ANGLES:
16°, 16°

VALVE TIMING:
62, 86, 86, 62

CLUTCH:
Borg and Beck

GEARBOX:
Hewland FG400

CHASSIS:
Lotus Aluminium Alloy Monocoque

FRONT SUSPENSION:
Double Wishbones, torsion bars

REAR SUSPENSION:
Parallel lower links, single top links, twin radius rods

DIMENSIONS:
Wheelbase   100 inches
Front and rear track 57 inches

ENGINE WEIGHT:
365 lb

GEARBOX WEIGHT:
98 lb

CHASSIS WEIGHT:
65 lb

COMPLETE CHAMPIONSHIP RACING RECORD OF THE LOTUS 72 ENTRIES, PRACTICE TIMES AND RESULTS 1971

DATE	EVENT	CAR AND CHASSIS NO.	NO.	DRIVER	PRACTICE 1	PRACTICE 2	PRACTICE 3	RACE RESULT
6 March 1971	South African G.P.	Lotus 72C/R5	2	Emerson Fittipaldi	1m 21.20s	1m 19.10s	1m 19.10s	Retired
6 March 1971	South African G.P.	Lotus 72C/R3	3	Reine Wisell	1m 21.40s	1m 20.20s	1m 19.90s	4th 1h 48m 44.90s
18 April 1971	Spanish G.P.	Lotus 72C/R5	2	Emerson Fittipaldi	1m 30.20s	1m 27.90s	1m 40.30s	Retired
18 April 1971	Spanish G.P.	Lotus 72C/R3	3	Reine Wisell	1m 31.50s	1m 28.60s	1m 41.20s	Not Classified
23 May 1971	Monaco G.P.	Lotus 72D/R5	1	Emerson Fittipaldi	1m 55.30s	1m 27.70s	1m 35.90s	5th
23 May 1971	Monaco G.P.	Lotus 72C/R3	2	Reine Wisell	1m 50.00s	1m 26.70s	1m 33.40s	Retired
20 June 1971	Dutch G.P.	Lotus 72D/R3	14	Reine Wisell	1m 18.70s	1m 45.83s	1m 19.58s	Disqualified
4 July 1971	French G.P.	Lotus 72D/R5	1	Emerson Fittipaldi	1m 54.54s	1m 54.22s	–	3rd 1h 47m 15.75s
4 July 1971	French G.P.	Lotus 72D/R3	2	Reine Wisell	1m 55.44s	1m 53.75s	–	6th 1h 47m 57.66s
17 July 1971	British G.P.	Lotus 72D/R5	1	Emerson Fittipaldi	1m 19.60s	1m 19.20s	1m 18.30s	3rd 1h 32m 22.00s
17 July 1971	British G.P.	Lotus 72D/R3	2	Dave Charlton	1m 21.20s	1m 20.72s	1m 20.05s	Retired
1 August 1971	German G.P.	Lotus 72D/R5	8	Emerson Fittipaldi	7m 43.00s	7m 32.70s	7m 27.50s	Retired
1 August 1971	German G.P.	Lotus 72D/R6	9	Reine Wisell	–	7m 45.40s	7m 39.96s	8th 1h 35m 47.40s
15 August 1971	Austrian G.P.	Lotus 72D/R5	2	Emerson Fittipaldi	1m 38.39s	1m 38.41s	1m 37.90s	2nd 1h 30m 28.03s
15 August 1971	Austrian G.P.	Lotus 72D/R6	3	Reine Wisell	1m 40.25s	1m 40.35s	1m 38.95s	4th 1h 30m 55.78s
19 September 1971	Canadian G.P.	Lotus 72D/R5	2	Emerson Fittipaldi	1m 18.60s	1m 18.30s	1m 16.10s	7th
19 September 1971	Canadian G.P.	Lotus 72D/R6	3	Reine Wisell	1m 20.00s	1m 16.80s	1m 16.30s	5th
3 October 1971	United States G.P.	Lotus 72D/R5	2	Emerson Fittipaldi	1m 43.87s	1m 42.66s	–	Not Classified
3 October 1971	United States G.P.	Lotus 72D/R6	3	Reine Wisell	1m 46.20s	1m 44.02s	–	Retired

CONSTRUCTORS' CUP

	MANUFACTURER	S.AFRICA	SPAIN	MONACO	HOLLAND	FRANCE	G.B.	GERMANY	AUSTRIA	ITALY	CANADA	USA	TOTAL
1.	Tyrell-Ford	6	9	9	–	9	9	9	–	4	9	9	73
2.	BRM	–	3	–	6	3	–	–	9	9	–	6	36
3.	Ferrari	9	6	4	9	–	–	4	–	–	–	1	33
3.	March-Ford	–	–	6	3	–	6	2	1	6	6	4	33
5.	Lotus-Ford	3	–	2	–	4	4	–	6	–	2	–	21
6.	McLaren-Ford	1	2	3	–	–	–	–	–	–	4	–	10
7.	Matra-Simca	2	4	–	–	2	–	–	–	1	–	–	9
8.	Surtees-Ford	–	–	1	2	–	2	–	–	3	–	–	8
9.	Brabham Ford	–	–	–	–	–	–	1	4	–	–	–	5

Results for the Constructors' Cup 1971 saw Lotus-Ford in 5th place with 21 points.

Type 72

Emerson Fittipaldi became the 1972 World Champion and headed off the challenge from Jackie Stewart. He did this with a racing record of five victories, two second place and one third place. This was against Jackie Stewart's four wins, one second place and one fourth place. Fittipaldi became the youngest ever World Champion at 25 in 1972. The opposite page shows the times in which he won at the Spanish Grand Prix, Belgian Grand Prix, European Grand Prix, Austrian Grand Prix and Italian Grand Prix. He headed the World Championship of Drivers for 1972 with 61 points. At the October World Championship victory meeting he received a hero's ovation at Brands Hatch touring in a Lotus Elan converted by Hexagon.

After a crash in practice at the Dutch G.P. 1973 and an injury, Emerson Fittipaldi had to make do with second place in 1973 though Lotus still headed the Constructor's Cup.

By 1974, Emerson Fittipaldi had moved to McLaren and became World Champion again. Lotus fell to fourth place in the Constructor's Cup 1974.

COMPLETE CHAMPIONSHIP RACING RECORD OF THE LOTUS 72 ENTRIES, PRACTICE TIMES AND RESULTS 1972

DATE EVENT		CAR AND	NO. CHASSIS NO.		DRIVER	PRACTICE 1	PRACTICE 2	PRACTICE 3	RACE RESULT	
23rd January 1972	Argentine G.P.	JPS Lotus 72D/R5	11	Emerson Fittipaldi	1m 14.32s	1m 13.28s	–	Retired	
23rd January 1972	Argentine G.P.	JPS Lotus 72D/R6	12	Dave Walker	1m 17.97s	1m 15.55s	–	Disqualified	
4th March 1972	South African G.P.	JPS Lotus 72D/R5	8	Emerson Fittipaldi	1m 17.90s	1m 17.40s	1m 17.40s	2nd	1h 46m 3.2s
4th March 1972	South African G.P.	JPS Lotus 72D/R6	9	Dave Walker	1m 18.80s	1m 18.10s	1m 17.90s	10th	1h 46m 57.9s
4th March 1972	South African G.P.	JPS Lotus 72D/R3	26	Dave Charlton	1m 26.10s	1m 18.50s	1m 19.40s	Retired	
1st May 1972	Spanish G.P.	JPS Lotus 72D/R7	5	Emerson Fittipaldi	1m 19.79s	1m 19.26s	–	1st	2h 3m 41.23s
1st May 1972	Spanish G.P.	JPS Lotus 72D/R5	21	Dave Walker	1m 23.82s	1m 22.74s	–	9th Not running	
14th May 1972	Monaco G.P.	JPS Lotus 72D/R7	8	Emerson Fittipaldi	1m 24.40s	1m 21.40s	1m 46.80s	3rd	
14th May 1972	Monaco G.P.	JPS Lotus 72D/R5	9	Dave Walker	1m 24.90s	1m 24.00s	1m 50.50s	14th	
4th June 1972	Belgian G.P.	JPS Lotus 72D/R7	32	Emerson Fittipaldi	1m 11.60s	1m 11.52s	1m 11.43s	1st	1h 44m 6.70s
4th June 1972	Belgian G.P.	JPS Lotus 72D/R6	33	Dave Walker	1m 13.30s	1m 13.30s	1m 12.76s	14th	
4th July 1972	French G.P.	JPS Lotus 72D/R7	1	Emerson Fittipaldi	3m 01.70s	2m 58.10s	–	2nd	1 h 44m 6.70s
4th July 1972	French G.P.	JPS Lotus 72D/R6	6	Dave Walker	3m 06.20s	3m 04.70s	–	18th Not running	
17th July 1972	European G.P.	JPS Lotus72D/R7	8	Emerson Fittipaldi	1m 26.40s	1m 22.90s	1m 23.70s	1st	1h 47m 50.20s
17th July 1972	European G.P.	JPS Lotus 72D/R6	9	Dave Walker	1m 25.40s	1m 25.80s	1m 25.10s	Retired	
17th July 1972	European G.P.	JPS Lotus 72D/R3	29	Dave Charlton	1m 29.90s	1m 26.80s	1m 26.30s	Retired	
1st August 1972	German G.P.	JPS Lotus 72D/R7	2	Emerson Fittipaldi	7m 21.91s	7m 14.90s	7m 09.90s	Retired	
1st August 1972	German G.P.	JPS Lotus 72D/R6	25	Dave Walker	7m 51.40s	–	7m 29.50s	Retired	
1st August 1972	German G.P.	JPS Lotus 72D/R3	29	Dave Charlton	8m 01.10s	7m 59.80s	7m 34.10s	Retired	
13th August 1972	Austrian G.P.	JPS Lotus 72D/R6	21	Dave Walker	1m 39.46s	1m 38.81s	–	Retired	
13th August 1972	Austrian G.P.	JPS Lotus 72D/R5	31	Emerson Fittipaldi	1m 35.97s	1m 36.69s	–	1st	1h 29m 16.66s
10th September 1972	Italian G.P.	JPS Lotus 72D/R5	6	Emerson Fittipaldi	1m 36.29s	1m 36.64s	–	1st	1h 29m 58.40s
24th September 1972	Canadian G.P.	JPS Lotus 72D/R7	5	Emerson Fittipaldi	1m 15.00s	1m 14.50s	1m 14.40s	11th	
24th September 1972	Canadian G.P.	JPS Lotus 72D/R6	6	Reine Wisell	1m 16.70s	1m 16.10s	1m 16.10s	Retired	
8th October 1972	United States G.P.	JPS Lotus 72D/R5	10	Emerson Fittipaldi	1m 42.40s	2m 24.80s	1m 55.70s	Retired	
8th October 1972	United States G.P.	JPS Lotus 72D/R7	11	Dave Walker	1m 50.60s	2m 22.10s	2m 04.57s	Retired	
8th October 1972	United States G.P.	JPS Lotus 72D/R6	12	Reine Wisell	1m 43.50s	2m 13.70s	1m 58.50s	10th	

CONSTRUCTORS CUP 1972

		ARGENTINA	S.AFRICA	SPAIN	MONACO	BELGIUM	FRANCE	G.B.	GERMANY	AUSTRIA	ITALY	CANADA	USA	TOTAL
1.	Lotus-Ford	–	6	9	4	9	6	9	–	9	9	–	–	61
2.	Tyrell--Ford	9	–	–	3	6	9	6	–	–	–	9	9	51
3.	McLaren-Ford	6	9	2	2	4	–	4	2	6	4	6	4	47
4.	Ferrari	4	3	6	6	–	–	1	9	–	–	2	2	33
5.	Surtees-Ford	2	–	3	–	3	1	–	–	3	6	–	–	18
6.	March-Ford	1	2	1	–	2	2	–	4	–	–	–	3	15
7.	BRM	–	–	–	9	–	–	–	3	1	1	–	–	14
8.	Matra Simca	–	–	–	1	1	4	3	–	2	–	1	–	12
9.	Brabham-Ford	–	1	–	–	–	–	–	1	–	2	3	–	7

Type 72

Emerson Fittipaldi in the Lotus 72 at the Rothmans 50,000, Brands Hatch on 28th August 1972. He won in a time of 2hrs 50 minutes 49.1 seconds.

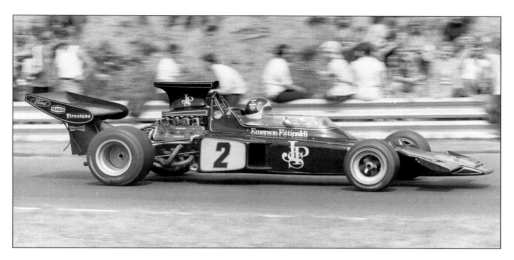

Emerson Fittipaldi at the 1972 German Grand Prix

RESULTS OF THE WORLD CHAMPIONSHIP 1972

POS	DRIVER	ARGENTINA	S.AFRICA	SPAIN	MONACO	BELGIUM	FRANCE	G.B.	GERMANY	AUSTRIA	ITALY	CANADA	USA	TOTAL
1.	Emerson Fittipaldi	–	6	9	4	9	6	9	–	9	9	–	–	61
2.	Jackie Stewart	9	–	–	3	–	9	6	–	–	–	9	9	45
3.	Danny Hulme	6	9	–	–	4	–	2	–	6	4	4	4	39
4.	Jacky Ickx	4	–	6	6	–	–	–	9	–	–	–	2	27
5.	Peter Revson	–	4	2	–	–	–	4	–	4	3	6	–	23
6.	Francois Cevert	–	–	–	–	6	3	–	–	–	–	–	6	15
7.	Clay Regazzoni	3	–	4	–	–	–	–	6	–	–	2	–	15
8.	Mike Hailwood	–	–	–	–	3	1	–	–	3	6	–	–	13
9.	Ronnie Peterson	1	2	–	–	–	2	–	4	–	–	–	3	12
10.	Chris Amon	–	–	–	1	1	4	3	–	2	–	1	–	12
11.	Jean-Pierre Beltoise	–	–	–	9	–	–	–	–	–	–	–	–	9
12.	Mario Andretti	–	3	–	–	–	–	–	–	–	–	–	1	4
12.	Howden Ganley	–	–	–	–	–	–	–	3	1	–	–	–	4
14.	Brian Redman	–	–	–	2	–	–	–	2	–	–	–	–	4
15.	Graham Hill	–	1	–	–	–	–	–	1	–	2	–	–	4
16.	Andrea de Adamich	–	–	3	–	–	–	–	–	–	–	–	–	3
16.	Carlos Reutemann	–	–	–	–	–	–	–	–	–	–	3	–	3
18.	Carlos Pace	–	–	1	–	2	–	–	–	–	–	–	–	3
19.	Tim Schenken	2	–	–	–	–	–	–	–	–	–	–	–	2
20.	Arturo Merzario	–	–	–	–	–	–	1	–	–	–	–	–	1
20.	Peter Gethin	–	–	–	–	–	–	–	–	–	1	–	–	1

Reine Wisell gained third place in the United States Grand Prix of 1970 in a Lotus 72C.

REINE WISELL RACING ENTRIES AND SUCCESSES

DATE	EVENT	DRIVER	CAR SPECIFICATION	CHASSIS NUMBER	RACE RESULT
4th October 1970	U.S. G.P.	R Wisell	72C	R3	3rd Place
25th October 1970	Mexican G.P.	R Wisell	72C	R3	10th Place
24th January 1971	Argentine G.P.	R Wisell	72C	R3	7th Place
6th March 1971	South African G.P.	R Wisell	72C	R3	4th Place
21st March 1971	Race of Champions	R Wisell	72C	R3	–
28th March 1971	Questor G.P.	R Wisell	72C	R3	–
18th April 1971	Spanish G.P.	R Wisell	72C	R3	12th Place
8th May 1971	International Trophy	R Wisell	72C	R3	–
23rd May 1971	Monaco G.P.	R Wisell	72C	R3	–
13th June 1971	Rindt Memorial Trophy	R Wisell	72D	R3	10th Place
20th June 1971	Dutch G.P.	R Wisell	72D	R3	–
4th July 1971	French G.P.	R Wisell	72D	R3	6th Place
1st August 1971	German G.P.	R Wisell	72D	R6	8th Place
15th August 1971	Austrian G.P.	R Wisell	72D	R6	4th Place
19th September 1971	Canadian G.P.	R Wisell	72D	R6	5th Place
3rd October 1971	U.S. G.P.	R Wisell	72D	R6	–
24th September 1972	Canadian G.P.	R Wisell	72D	R6	–
8th October 1972	U. S. G.P.	R Wisell	72D	R6	10th Place

TYPE 72

1973 saw the appointment of Ralph Bellamy as Lotus chief designer while Eddie Dennis remained chief mechanic. Ronnie Peterson made his first appearance for Team Lotus at the Argentine Grand Prix in "no. 4" but retired.

Emerson Fittipaldi's winning start to the season included the Argentine Grand Prix in a time of 1hour 55 minutes 18.22 seconds, and the Spanish Grand Prix in a time of 1 hour 48 minutes 18.7 seconds. The Spanish Grand Prix represented three Grand Prix wins from four races but things soon began to go wrong. A crash in practice at the 1973 Dutch Grand Prix meant the end of the road for Emerson's "72/5" car when it hit barriers at high speed. This left Ronnie Peterson as the only driver with a spare car. At the end of the 1973 season Eddie Dennis who had been chief mechanic for three seasons decided to take a job back at the Lotus factory.

At the Italian Grand Prix in 1973 Fittipaldi lost his World Championship title to Jackie Stewart while team mate Ronnie Peterson was becoming a joint number one with Fittipaldi at Lotus. Near the end of the 1973 season, Emerson Fittipaldi, wooed heavily by Marlboro, decided to leave Lotus for McLaren. Fittipaldi had been influenced by the fact that Marlboro were a huge company and that many of his toughest races in 1973 had been against McLarens.

Dave Walker (above) was signed as number two to Emerson Fittipaldi for 1972. But Walker's ten starts bought him seven did not finish's all due to mechanical failure. Walker's mechanics Rex Hart and Steve May denied Walker was given inferior equipment. But Peter Warr has conceded that Emerson Fittipaldi's number one status penalised Walker and "If there were any development bits, Emerson would get them"

COMPLETE CHAMPIONSHIP RACING RECORD OF THE LOTUS 72 ENTRIES, PRACTICE TIMES AND RESULTS 1973

DATE	EVENT	CAR AND CHASSIS NO.	NO.	DRIVER	PRACTICE 1	PRACTICE 2	PRACTICE 3	RACE RESULT
28th January 1973	Argentine G.P.	JPS Lotus 72D/R7	2	Emerson Fittipaldi	1m 11.87s	1m 11.18s	1m 11.87s	1st 1h 56m 18.22s
28th January 1973	Argentine G.P.	JPS Lotus 72D/R8	4	Ronnie Peterson	1m 14.08s	–	1m 11.87s	Retired
11th February 1973	Brazilian G.P.	JPS Lotus 72D/R7	1	Emerson Fittipaldi	2m 31.60s	2m 31.50s	2m 34.30s	1st 1h 43m 55.60s
11th February 1973	Brazilian G.P.	JPS Lotus 72D/R8	2	Ronnie Peterson	2m 31.50s	2m 30.50s	2m 34.00s	Retired
3rd March 1973	South African G.P.	JPS Lotus 72D/R7	1	Emerson Fittipaldi	1m 17.00s	1m 16.65s	1m 16.41s	3rd 1h 43m 36.13s
3rd March 1973	South African G.P.	JPS Lotus 72D/R8	2	Ronnie Peterson	1m 17.04s	1m 16.44s	1m 16.55s	11th
3rd March 1973	South African G.P.	JPS Lotus 72D/R3	25	Dave Charlton	1m 30.29s	1m 19.73s	1m 17.18s	Retired
29th April 1973	Spanish G.P.	JPS Lotus 72D/R5	1	Emerson Fittipaldi	–	–	1m 23.70s	1st 1h 48m 18.70s
29th April 1973	Spanish G.P.	JPS Lotus 72D/R8	2	Ronnie Peterson	1m 22.40s	1m 21.80s	1m 21.80s	Retired
20th May 1973	European G.P.	JPS Lotus 72D/R7	1	Emerson Fittipaldi	1m 26.08s	1m 24.23s	1m 23.44s	3rd 1h 44m 16.22s
20th May 1973	European G.P.	JPS Lotus 72D/R6	2	Ronnie Peterson	1m 27.31s	1m 23.05s	1m 22.46s	Retired
3rd June 1973	Monaco G.P.	JPS Lotus 72D/R7	1	Emerson Fittipaldi	1m 31.90s	1m 28.10s	1m 28.90s	2nd 1h 57m 45.60s
3rd June 1973	Monaco G.P.	JPS Lotus 72D/R6	2	Ronnie Peterson	1m 28.80s	1m 27.70s	1m 35.20s	3rd
17th June 1973	Swedish G.P.	JPS Lotus 72D/R7	1	Emerson Fittipaldi	1m 25.70s	1m 24.70s	1m 24.10s	12th Not running
17th June 1973	Swedish G.P.	JPS Lotus 72D/R6	2	Ronnie Peterson	1m 24.80s	1m 23.10s	–	2nd 1h 56m 50.09s
1st July 1973	French G.P.	JPS Lotus 72D/R5	1	Emerson Fittipaldi	1m 51.00s	1m 50.09s	1m 49.36s	Retired
1st July 1973	French G.P.	JPS Lotus 72D/R6	2	Ronnie Peterson	1m 49.45s	1m 50.64s	1m 49.64s	1st 1h 41m 36.52s
14th July 1973	British G.P.	JPS Lotus 72D/R5	1	Emerson Fittipaldi	1m 16.90s	1m 16.70s	–	Retired
14th July 1973	British G.P.	JPS Lotus 72D/R6	2	Ronnie Peterson	–	1m 16.30s	–	2nd 1h 29m 21.30s
29th July 1973	Dutch G.P.	JPS Lotus 72D/R7	1	Emerson Fittipaldi	–	–	–	Retired
29th July 1973	Dutch G.P.	JPS Lotus 72D/R6	2	Ronnie Peterson	1m 36.01s	1m 30.00s	1m 21.38s	11th not running
5th August 1973	German G.P.	JPS Lotus 72D/R7	1	Emerson Fittipaldi	7m 19.70s	7m 20.00s	–	6th 1h 43m 27.3s
5th August 1973	German G.P.	JPS Lotus 72D/R6	2	Ronnie Peterson	7m 08.30s	7m 20.60s	–	Retired
19th August 1973	Austrian G.P.	JPS Lotus 72D/R7	1	Emerson Fittipaldi	1m 37.01s	11m 36.71s	1m 36.55s	11th not running
19th August 1973	Austrian G.P.	JPS Lotus 72D/R6	2	Ronnie Peterson	1m 39.10s	1m 35.37s	1m 38.42s	1st 1h 28m 48.78s
9th September 1973	Italian G.P.	JPS Lotus 72D/R7	1	Emerson Fittipaldi	1m 39.43s	1m 38.76s	1m 36.26s	2nd 1h 29m 17.80s
9th September 1973	Italian G.P.	JPS Lotus 72D/R6	2	Ronnie Peterson	1m 42.22s	1m 36.79s	1m 36.08s	1st 1h 29m 17.00s
23rd September 1973	Canadian G.P.	JPS Lotus 72D/R7	1	Emerson Fittipaldi	1m 16.07s	1m 15.84s	1m 15.04s	1st 1h 59m 36.82
23rd September 1973	Canadian G.P.	JPS Lotus 72D/R6	2	Ronnie Peterson	1m 14.65s	1m 13.70s	1m 14.59s	Retired
7th October 1973	United States G.P.	JPS Lotus 72D/R7	1	Emerson Fittipaldi	1m 42.01s	1m 40.39s	1m 41.45s	6th 1h 43m 3.75s
7th October 1973	United States G.P.	JPS Lotus 72D/R6	2	Ronnie Peterson	2m 02.97s	1m 39.66s	1m 41.68s	1st 1h 41m 15.78s

Lotus 72

RESULTS OF THE WORLD CHAMPIONSHIP 1973

POS	DRIVER	ARGENTINA	BRAZIL	S.AFRICA	SPAIN	BELGIUM	MONACO	SWEDEN	FRANCE	FRANCE	HOLLAND	GERMANY	AUSTRIA	ITALY	CANADA	USA	TOTAL
1.	Jackie Stewart	4	6	9	–	9	9	2	3	–	9	9	6	3	2	–	71
2.	Emerson Fittipaldi	9	9	4	9	4	6	–	–	–	–	1	–	6	6	1	55
3.	Ronnie Peterson	–	–	–	–	–	4	6	9	6	–	–	9	29	–	9	52
4.	Francois Cevert	6	–	–	6	6	3	4	6	2	6	6	–	2	–	–	47
5.	Peter Revson	–	–	6	3	–	2	–	–	9	3	–	–	4	9	2	38
6.	Denny Hulme	2	4	2	1	–	1	9	–	4	–	–	–	–	–	3	26
7.	Carlos Reutemann	–	–	–	–	–	–	3	4	1	–	–	3	1	–	4	16
8.	James Hunt	–	–	–	–	–	–	–	1	3	4	–	–	–	–	6	14
9.	Jacky Ickx	3	2	–	–	–	–	1	2	–	–	4	–	–	–	–	12
10.	Jean-Pierre Beltoise	–	–	–	2	–	–	–	–	–	2	–	2	–	3	–	9
11.	Carlos Pace	–	–	–	–	–	–	–	–	–	–	3	4	–	–	–	7
12.	Arturo Merzario	–	3	3	–	–	–	–	–	–	–	–	–	–	–	–	6
13.	George Follmer	–	–	1	4	–	–	–	–	–	–	–	–	–	–	–	5
14.	Jackie Oliver	–	–	–	–	–	–	–	–	–	–	–	–	–	4	–	4
15.	Andrea de Adamich	–	–	–	–	3	–	–	–	–	–	–	–	–	–	–	3
16.	Wilson Fittipaldi	1	–	–	–	–	–	–	–	–	–	2	–	–	–	–	3
17.	Niki Lauda	–	–	–	–	2	–	–	–	–	–	–	–	–	–	–	2
18.	Clay Regazzoni	–	1	–	–	–	–	–	–	–	–	–	1	–	–	–	2
19.	Chris Amon	–	–	–	–	1	–	–	–	–	–	–	–	–	–	–	1
19.	Gijs van Lennep	–	–	–	–	–	–	–	–	–	1	–	–	–	–	–	1
19.	Howden Ganley	–	–	–	–	–	–	–	–	–	–	–	–	–	1	–	1

RESULTS OF THE WORLD CHAMPIONSHIP 1974

POS	MANUFACTURER	ARGENTINA	BRAZIL	S.AFRICA	SPAIN	BELGIUM	MONACO	SWEDEN	FRANCE	NETHERLANDS	GERMANY	AUSTRIA	ITALY	CANADA	G.B.	USA	TOTAL
1.	Emerson Fittipaldi	–9	–	4	9	2	3	–	4	–	–	6	9	6	3	–	55
2.	Clay Reggazoni	4	6	–	6	3	3	–	4	6	9	2	–	6	3	–	52
3.	Jody Schekter	–	–	–	2	4	6	9	3	2	6	–	4	–	9	–	45
4.	Niki Lauda	6	–	–	9	6	–	–	6	9	–	–	–	–	2	–	38
5.	Ronnie Peterson	–	1	–	–	–	9	–	9	–	3	–	9	–	4	–	35
6.	Carlos Reutemann	–	–	9	–	–	–	–	–	–	4	9	–	–	1	9	32
7.	Denny Hulme	9	–	–	1	1	–	–	1	–	–	6	1	1	–	–	20
8.	James Hunt	–	–	–	–	–	–	4	–	–	–	4	–	3	–	4	15
9.	Patrick Depallier	1	–	3	–	–	–	6	–	1	–	–	–	2	–	1	14
10.	Jacky Ickx	–	4	–	–	–	–	–	2	–	2	–	–	–	4	–	12
10.	Mike Hailwood	3	2	4	–	–	–	–	–	3	–	–	–	–	–	–	12
12.	Carlos Pace	–	3	–	–	–	–	–	–	–	–	–	2	–	–	6	11
13.	Jean-Peirre Beltoise	2	–	6	–	2	–	–	–	–	–	–	–	–	–	–	10
14.	Jean-Pierre Jarrier	–	–	–	–	–	4	2	–	–	–	–	–	–	–	–	6
14.	John Watson	–	–	–	–	–	1	–	–	–	–	2	–	–	–	2	6
16.	Hans-Joachim Stuck	–	–	2	3	–	–	–	–	–	–	–	–	–	–	–	5
17.	Arturo Merzaro	–	–	1	–	–	–	–	–	–	–	–	3	–	–	–	4
18	Graham Hill	–	–	–	–	–	1	–	–	–	–	–	–	–	–	–	1
18.	Tom Pryce	–	–	–	–	–	–	–	–	–	1	–	–	–	–	–	1
18.	Vittorio Brambilla	–	–	–	–	–	–	–	–	–	–	1	–	–	–	–	1

LOTUS 72

The Grand Prix season started early in 1974, the first race being the Argentine Grand Prix on 12th January. The drivers were Ronnie Peterson and Jacky Ickx and their cars were 72/8 and 72/5 respectively. In late 1973 Team Lotus had sold two Lotus 72's to Team Gunston in South Africa for Ian Scheckter and Paddy Driver. Consequently neither Ronnie Peterson nor Jacky Ickx had a spare car so any serious accident was likely to mean withdrawal. The start to the 1974 season was dissapointing with Ronnie Peterson coming thirteenth and Jacky Ickx retiring.

At the South African Grand Prix of 1974 both Ronnie Peterson and Jacky Ickx had driven the new Lotus 76 but Ickx retired while Peterson's car was in an accident. For the Spanish Grand Prix Peterson and Ickx again drove the new Lotus 76 but Peterson retired with an overheated engine while Ickx retired with leaking brake fluid. Worse still this was after just 23 and 26 laps respectively. The problem had been that testing the Lotus 76 had been done mainly at Grand Prix events themselves. At the Belgian Grand Prix Peterson and Ickx again drove the Lotus 76s, Peterson retiring with a leaking fuel pump and Ickx retiring with brake problems.

Reverting to the Lotus 72 for the Monaco Grand Prix, despite the high profile launch of the Lotus 76, paid dividends. Ronnie Peterson won the 1974 Monaco Grand Prix in a time of 1 hour 58 minutes and 3.7 seconds. He had already set the record for fastest lap of 1 minute 27.9 seconds.

JPS/ LOTUS 72 OF 1974

SPONSOR:
John Player-Duckhams

ENGINE:

Type	Cosworth DFV
Bore and stroke	85.6 mm x 64.8 mm
Capacity	2933 cc
Maximum power	460 bhp at 10,250 rpm
Valve sizes	1.32 inches x 2
	1.14 inches x 2
Valve lift	0.4 inches
Valve timing	62, 86, 86, 62
Pistons and rings	Cosworth-Hepolite
Bearings	Vandervell

SUSPENSION DAMPERS:
Koni

WHEEL DIAMETER:
13 inches front and rear

TYRES:
Goodyear

RADIATOR:
Serck

FUEL TANKS:
marston excelsior cells

WHEELBASE:
100 inches

ENGINE WEIGHT:
365 lbs

GEARBOX WEIGHT:
103 lbs

FUEL CONSUMPTION:
6.2 mpg

COMPLETE CHAMPIONSHIP RACING RECORD OF THE LOTUS 72 ENTRIES, PRACTICE TIMES AND RESULTS 1974

DATE	EVENT	CAR AND CHASSIS NO.	NO.	DRIVER	PRACTICE 1	PRACTICE 2	PRACTICE 3	RACE RESULT
13th January 1974	Argentine G.P.	JPS Lotus 72E/R8	1	Ronnie Peterson	1m 54.36s	1m 52.28s	1m 53.00s	13th
13th January 1974	Argentine G.P.	JPS Lotus 72E/R5	2	Jacky Ickx	1m 54.73s	1m 53.64s	1m 54.16s	Retired
27th January 1974	Brazilian G.P.	JPS Lotus 72E/R8	1	Ronnie Peterson	2m 34.10s	2m 32.82s	2m 34.38s	6th 1h 23m 03.34s
27th January 1974	Brazilian G.P.	JPS Lotus 72E/R5	2	Jacky Ickx	2m 36.10s	2m 35.30s	2m 34.64s	3rd 1h 22m 06.70s
30th March 1974	South African G.P.	Gunston Lotus 72E/R6	29	Ian Scheckter	1m 18.56s	1m 20.07s	–	13th 1h 43m 13.31s
30th March 1974	South African G.P.	Gunston Lotus 72E/R7	30	Paddy Driver	1m 19.49s	1m 20.98s	–	Retired
26th May 1974	Monaco G.P.	JPS Lotus 72E/R8	1	Ronnie Peterson	1m 29.50s	1m 26.80s	1m 26.80s	1st 1h 58m 3.70s
26th May 1974	Monaco G.P.	JPS Lotus 72E/R5	2	Jacky Ickx	1m 38.60s	1m 29.40s	1m 29.50s	Retired
9th June 1974	Swedish G.P.	JPS Lotus 72E/R8	1	Ronnie Peterson	1m 27.44s	1m 29.19s	1m 25.54s	Retired
9th June 1974	Swedish G.P.	JPS Lotus 72E/R5	2	Jacky Ickx	1m 29.79s	1m 33.12s	1m 25.65s	Retired
23rd June 1974	Dutch G.P.	JPS Lotus 72E/R8	1	Ronnie Peterson	1m 20.22s	1m 20.23s	1m 21.55s	8th 1h 43m 21.49s
23rd June 1974	Dutch G.P.	JPS Lotus 72E/R5	2	Jacky Ickx	–	1m 21.21s	1m 22.28s	11th 1h 43m 14.32s
7th July 1974	French G.P.	JPS Lotus 72E/R8	1	Ronnie Peterson	1m 0.61s	0m 59.28s	0m 59.27s	1st 1h 21m 55.02s
7th July 1974	French G.P.	JPS Lotus 72E/R5	2	Jacky Ickx	1m 1.48s	1m 00.31s	1m 00.55s	5th 1h 22m 32.56s
20th July 1974	British G.P.	JPS Lotus 72E/R8	1	Ronnie Peterson	1m 22.10s	1m 20.60s	1m 21.70s	10th 1h 43m 18.10s
20th July 1974	British G.P.	JPS Lotus 72E/R5	2	Jacky Ickx	1m 23.10s	1m 22.10s	1m 21.20s	3rd 1h 44m 03.70s
4th August 1974	German G.P.	JPS Lotus 72E/R5	2	Jacky Ickx	1m 09.10s	1m 12.70s	–	5th 1h 43m 0.05s
18th August 1974	Austrian G.P.	JPS Lotus 72E/R8	1	Ronnie Peterson	1m 38.43s	1m 37.45s	1m 37.07s	Retired
8th September 1974	Italian G.P.	JPS Lotus 72E/R8	1	Ronnie Peterson	–	1m 34 24s	1m 35.44s	1st 1h 22m 56.60s
22nd September 1974	Canadian G.P.	JPS Lotus 72E/R8	1	Ronnie Peterson	1m 15.90s	1m 15.30s	1m 19.73s	3rd 1h 40m 40.63s
22nd September 1974	Canadian G.P.	JPS Lotus 72E/R5	2	Jacky Ickx	1m 21.00s	–	1m 15.67s	13th 1h 40m 52.62s
6th October 1974	United States G.P.	JPS Lotus 72E/R8	1	Ronnie Peterson	1m 41.99s	1m 41.35s	1m 41.92s	Retired
6th October 1974	United States G.P.	JPS Lotus 72E/R5	2	Jacky Ickx	1m 41.72s	1m 40.88s	1m 43.44s	Retired

Ronnie Peterson won at the Monaco Grand Prix, the French Grand Prix and the Italian Grand Prix but is only 5th in the 1974 World Championship of Drivers. Lotus were down to 4th place on the Constructors' title.

LOTUS 72

Ronnie Peterson and Jacky Ickx were again the drivers for the Lotus 72 in 1975, Peterson having signed a contract for the 1975 and 1976 seasons back in 1974 and Ickx having joined for two seasons when he started at the end of 1973. Peterson retained 72/8 and Ickx retained 72/5.

Before the South African Grand Prix Lotus finished building chassis 72/9, and in the South African Grand Prix the Gunston Lotus 72's of Eddie Keizan and Guy Tunmer were also entered. In the race itself Peterson came 10th, Ickx came 12th, Keizan came 13th and Tunmer came 11th. Cars that Colin Chapman had sold at the end of 1973 had virtually matched the performance of the works cars in this particular Grand Prix. At the Daily Mail Race of Champions Ronnie Peterson had his new car, chassis 72/9 and finished in fourth, with Jacky Ickx finishing fifth.

Jacky Ickx was second in the Spanish Grand Prix in a time of 42 minutes 54.8 seconds. Jacky Ickx had been unhappy with both his own performance and that of an ageing design (the Lotus 72) and left after the French Grand Prix. Brian Henton was to be his replacement. Ickx was allowed to drive for any other team until the appearance of the Lotus 77.

CONSTRUCTORS CUP 1975

POS	MANUFACTURER	ARGENTINA	BRAZIL	S. AFRICA	SPAIN	MONACO	BELGIUM	SWEDEN	NETHERLANDS	FRANCE	G.B.	GERMANY	AUSTRIA	ITALY	U.S.A	TOTAL
1.	Ferrari	3	3	2	–	9	9	9	6	9	–	4	0.5	9	9	72.5
2.	Brabham-Cosworth	4	9	6	2	4	4	6	3	–	6	9	–	3	–	54
3.	McLaren-Cosworth	9	6	1	4.5	6	–	–	–	4	9	–	1.5	3	–	53
4.	Hesketh-Cosworth	6	1	–	–	–	–	–	9	6	3	–	3	2	3	33
5.	Tyrell-Cosworth	2	–	9	–	2	6	–	–	1	4	–	–	–	1	25
6.	Shadow-Cosworth	–	–	–	1.5	–	1	–	1	–	–	3	2	1	–	9.5
7.	Lotus-Cosworth	–	–	–	3	3	–	–	–	–	–	–	1	–	2	9
8.	March-Cosworth	–	–	–	1	–	–	–	–	–	2	–	4.5	–	–	7.5
9.	Williams-Cosworth	–	–	–	–	–	–	–	–	–	–	6	–	–	–	6
10.	Parnelli-Cosworth	–	–	–	–	–	–	–	3	–	2	–	–	–	–	5
11.	Hill-Cosworth	–	–	–	–	–	–	–	1	–	–	2	–	–	–	3
12.	Penske-Cosworth	–	–	–	–	–	–	–	2	–	–	–	–	–	–	2
13.	Ensign-Cosworth	–	–	–	–	–	–	–	–	–	–	1	–	–	–	1

Lotus were 7th in the Constructor's Cup while Ronnie Peterson was joint 12th driver for 1975.

COMPLETE CHAMPIONSHIP RACING RECORD OF THE LOTUS 72 ENTRIES, PRACTICE TIMES AND RESULTS 1975

DATE	EVENT	CAR AND CHASSIS NO.	NO.	DRIVER	PRACTICE 1	PRACTICE 2	Practice 3	Race result
12th January 1975	Argentine Grand Prix	JPS Lotus 72E/R8	5	Ronnie Peterson	1m 51.82s	1m 51.65ss	1' 51.98s	Retired
12th January 1975	Argentine Grand Prix	JPS Lots 72E/R5	6	Jacky Ickx	1m 53.23s	1m 53.76s	1m 53.15s	8th 1h 39m 58.24s
26th January 1975	Brazilian Grand Prix	JPS Lotus 72E/R8	5	Ronnie Peterson	2m 37.81s	3m 9.93s	2m 34.25s	15th
26th January 1975	Brazilian Grand Prix	JPS Lotus 72E/R5	6	Jacky Ickx	2m 35.50s	2m 33.20s	2m 35.58s	9th 1h 46m 33.01s
1st March 1975	South African Grand Prix	JPS Lotus 72E/R9	5	Ronnie Peterson	1m 19.00s	1m 18.20s	1m 18.06s	10th
1st March 1975	South African Grand Prix	JPS Lotus 72E/R5	6	Jacky Ickx	1m 19.47s	1m 19.03s	1m 19.46s	12th
27th April 1975	Spanish Grand Prix	JPS Lotus 72E/R9	5	Ronnie Peterson	–	–	1m 25.30s	Retired
27th April 1975	Spanish Grand Prix	JPS Lotus 72E/R5	6	Jacky Ickx	1m 32.10s	1m 28.60s	1m 26.30s	2nd 42m 54.8s
11th May 1975	Monaco Grand Prix	JPS Lotus 72E/R9	5	Ronnie Peterson	1m 27.93s	1m 29.13s	1m 27.40s	4th 2h 1m 59.76s
11th May 1975	Monaco Grand Prix	JPS Lotus 72E/R5	6	Jacky Ickx	1m 29.95s	1m 29.02s	1m 28.28s	8th
25th May 1975	Belgian Grand Prix	JPS Lotus 72E/R9	5	Ronnie Peterson	1m 28.52s	1m 27.47s	1m 36.02s	Retired
25th May 1975	Belgian Grand Prix	JPS Lotus 72E/R5	6	Jacky Ickx	1m 29.19s	1m 28.45s	1m 35.64s	Retired
8th June 1975	Swedish Grand Prix	JPS Lotus 72E/R9	5	Ronnie Peterson	1m 26.41s	1m 26.01s	1m 26.25s	9th 2h 0m 10.46s
8th June 1975	Swedish Grand Prix	JPS Lotus 72E/R5	6	Jacky Ickx	1m 28.40s	1m 27.32s	1m 29.94s	15th 1h 59m 39.04s
22nd June 1975	Dutch Grand Prix	JPS Lotus 72E/R9	5	Ronnie Peterson	1m 22.22s	1m 22.48s	1m 21.90s	Retired
22nd June 1975	Dutch Grand Prix	JPS Lotus 72E/R5	6	Jacky Ickx	1m 23.20s	1m 23.76s	1m 23.26s	Retired
6th July 1975	French Grand Prix	JPS Lotus 72E/R9	5	Ronnie Peterson	1m 50.73s	–	1m 50.26s	10th 1h 41m 54.86s
6th July 1975	French Grand Prix	JPS Lotus 72E/R5	6	Jacky Ickx	1m 51.89s	1m 52.34s	1m 51.36s	Retired
19th July 1975	British Grand Prix	JPS Lotus 72E/R9	5	Ronnie Peterson	1m 20.6s	1m 20.60s	1m 22.30s	Retired
19th July 1975	British Grand Prix	JPS Lotus 72F/R8	6	Jim Crawford	1m 22.60s	1m 21.90s	1m 22.10s	Retired
19th July 1975	British Grand Prix	JPS Lotus 72F/R5	15	Brian Henton	1m 22.10s	1m 21.50s	1m 21.40s	16th 1h 20m 31.8s
3rd August 1975	German Grand Prix	JPS Lotus 72E/R9	5	Ronnie Peterson	7m 13.30s	–	7m 11.60s	Retired
3rd August 1975	German Grand Prix	JPS Lotus 72F/R8	6	John Watson	7m 14.10s	1m 13.30s	7m 9.40s	Retired
17th August 1975	Austrian Grand Prix	JPS Lotus 72E/R9	5	Ronnie Peterson	1m 37.61s	–	1m 37.70s	5th 59m 20.02s
7th September 1975	Italian Grand Prix	JPS Lotus 72E/R9	5	Ronnie Peterson	1m 35.19s	1m 35.39s	1m 34.51s	Retired
7th September 1975	Italian Grand Prix	JPS Lotus 72F/R8	6	Jim Crawford	1m 38.95s	1m 38.34s	1m 37.23s	13th
5th October 1975	United States Grand Prix	JPS Lotus 72E/R9	5	Ronnie Peterson	1m 45.75s	1m 44.54s	1m 43.57s	5th 1h 43m 48.16s
5th October 1975	United States Grand Prix	JPS Lotus 72F/R5	6	Brian Henton	1m 50.29s	1m 47.13s	1m 45.24s	Running not classified

Club Lotus Australia
PO Box 220, Strathfield,
New South Wales,
2135 Australia
Tel: +61 (0) 2 6521598

Club Lotus N.Z. Inc
Contact: Warwick Chandler
PO Box 27-016,
Mt Roskill, Auckland
New Zealand
Tel: +64 (0) 9 638 9551

Club Lotus Portugal
Pr. Afonso V,
120, Porto P-4150-024,
Portugal
Tel: +35 1 2618 2028
Fax: +35 1 2618 2028

Club Team Lotus Belgium V.Z.W
Contact: Daniel Absil
Molierelaan 505,
Brussel, B-1050,
Belgium
Tel: +32 (0) 2 345 75 70
Fax: +32 (0) 2 640 3943

Historical Lotus Register
Badgers Farm, Short Green,
Winfarthing, Norfolk
IP22 2EE, England
Tel: +44 (0) 1953 860 508

Lotus Car Club of Great British Columbia
Contact: Stephen Harpen
PO BOx 125, 3456 Dunbar Street,
Vancouver, British Columbia,
V6S 2C2, Canada
Email: stephen@bcsympatico.ca

Lotus Club Holland
Contact: Jean-Claude Brachmond
24 am Floss, Diekirch,
9232, Luxembourg
Tel: +352 80 91 48
Fax: +352 80 91 48

Lotus Drivers Club
56a Beverley Gardens,
St Albans, Hertfordshire
AL4 9BJ, England
Tel: +44 (0) 1727 838015
Fax: +44 (0) 1386 792720

Lotus Limited
PO Box L, College Park,
Maryland, MD20741, USA
Tel: +1 (301) 982-4054
Email: lotusltd@lotuscarclub.org

Lotus Seven Club
Contact: Julie Richens
PO Box 7, Cranleigh,
Surrey GU6 8YF, England
Tel: +44 (0) 1483 277172
Fax: +44 (0) 1483 277172
Email: nickandjulie@compuserve.com

North American Lotus Eleven Register
16 Madoc Street, Newton Centre,
Massachusetts, MA 02159, USA
Tel: +1 (617) 965 2058
Fax:+1 (617) 965 0761

North East Lotus Owners
1 Biddick Villas, Columbia Village,
Washington, Tyne & Wear,
NE38 7DT, England
Tel: +44 (0) 191 417 3005

Golden Fate Lotus Club
PO Box 117303, Burlingame,
California, USA, 94011
Email: gglcmail@gglotus.org

Club Lotus Austria
Mauer Hauptplatz 10,
A-1230 Vienna, Austria
Email: lotus@triform.at
Fax: 0043 (1) 548 23 40

Swiss Lotus Club
Contact: E.Schwyn
Industriestr 40,
CH-8152, Glarttbrugg

Lotus Club Deutschland
President: Felix Maria Arnet, Hugo Schneider
Address: Im Hopfengarten 11b,
65207 Wiesbaden
Tel: +44 6127/96 79 06
Fax: +49 6127/96 79 08
E-mail: Felix Maria Arnet
www.lotus-club-deutschland.de

Lotus Klub Danmark
President: Bo Stonor Johansen
Address: Jorgan Jensen,
Lillemarken 1, Gevninge,
4000, Roskilde
Tel: +45 64602232

Evergreen Lotus Car Club
PO Box 40481 Bellevue,
WA98015-4481
www.elcc.org

Club Lotus Northwest
PO Box 541, Oregan City,
OR 97045, USA

Lotus Club Canada
c/o Don Horne
20 Edgecliff Drive, #403,
Don Mills, Ontario,
M3C 3A4, Canada
Email: don.horne@2web.net